TECHNIQUES FOR
MANAGING

Verbally and Physically Aggressive Students

BEVERLEY H. JOHNS

VALERIE G. CARR

Garrison Alternative School
Jacksonville, Illinois

LOVE PUBLISHING COMPANY®

Denver · London · Sydney

Library of Congress Catalog Card Number 95-75400

Copyright © 1995 Love Publishing Company
Printed in the U.S.A.
ISBN 0-89108-240-9

*To Lonnie and Doug,
whose patience, support,
fortitude, and partnership
make our work possible.*

CONTENTS

PREFACE

*A*cts of crime and violence are increasing in U.S. schools. Today teachers and administrators must deal with more verbal and physical aggression than ever before. Long (1992), reporting on the unparalleled increase in school violence over the past five years, noted that in one academic year 2.4 million students had property stolen at school, 400,000 students were victims of assault, and 1 out of 20 reported being frightened they would be intimidated by a bully during the day. A recent newsletter headline read: "Gun fights are replacing fist fights in schools!" (cited in Long, 1992).

The problem is no longer limited to urban schools; it also exists in rural areas across the country. It is reaching epidemic proportions.

Teachers and administrators can no longer use the disciplinary techniques that they used twenty years ago. Paddling and suspending or expelling students are not effective methods for stemming the tide of violence. School staff must change their ways of dealing with students if schools are to once again be safe havens for children.

This book provides practical suggestions for dealing with verbally and physically aggressive students. The suggestions are based on our many years of experience in working with children with severe behavioral problems. It is our belief that techniques that have proven effective with this population will also be successful with the general education population.

Beverley H. Johns
Valerie G. Carr

 **REFERENCES**

Long, N. (1992). Managing a shooting incident. *Journal of Emotional and Behavioral Problems, 1*(1), 23–26.

DEVELOPING THE MINDSET OF CONFLICT AS A MANAGEABLE CHALLENGE

1

*E*ducation in the 20th century has witnessed massive change, the most dramatic of which has been the rise in aggression within the school setting. Not only must schools grapple with this problem from an administrative standpoint but teachers and professionals dealing with students in the classroom setting must also examine their roles in dealing with verbal and physical aggression.

When one looks at the characteristics of teachers who successfully manage and teach difficult students, one striking quality frequently becomes evident. These individuals do not allow a negative mindset to control their interactions with students. Rather than viewing their students as "miserable little monsters," they see each student as a person worth their time. They adhere to a mindset that recognizes human worth and potential. By no means do they overlook inappropriate behaviors. To the contrary, they treat students firmly and fairly and consistently enforce expectations, thereby creating safe and secure classrooms in which the priority is learning and the dominant attitude is respect.

Their mindset reflects characteristics commonly contained in quality mission statements, specifically the belief in the potential of every student, in their positive attributes, and in their ability to become productive citizens. Teachers who view students with this mindset generally recognize that in the 20th century their job has gone beyond imparting only academic information to students. They recognize that some students lack the skills to deal with frustration, have self esteem significantly below average, and use verbal and physical aggression as their first and often only means of defense. These teachers recognize that not all students come to them "ready to learn."

Teachers sensitive to the needs of the verbally and physically aggressive students utilize a positive, proactive approach when dealing with these students. They analyze the students' problem behaviors using general problem-solving techniques. Stepping back from a problem behavior, they rethink and analyze the circumstances. They request help when needed, seeking opinions and ideas from others. Then they generate a number of solutions and select and implement strategies for improvement. They continually monitor and evaluate classroom situations, revising their strategies as needed. These teachers plan ahead for behavioral needs. Even when their plans and interventions do not work they know that they have made a positive effort for their students.

We believe that every teacher is part of the process of academic and behavioral learning for each student. The analogy of links in a chain can be used, especially with the concept of behavior management. For the aggressive student, each positive adult is an important link in the chain. Although progress may not emerge for months or years, the input of each adult strengthens the chance that the aggressive student will make positive behavior changes. Teachers need to view positive behavior intervention as laying the groundwork for change. Each positive effort forges another solid link in the chain of behavioral change.

Teachers must view conflict as a manageable challenge and behavior management as an integral part of teaching. This mindset allows them to be more flexible in the teaching process. Those teachers who are prepared for the disruptive student can deal with problem behaviors and continue teaching. They do not get caught up in the behavioral situation. They can often circumvent problems by displaying firm, fair, and consistent enforcement of expectations. Those teachers who are unprepared for and easily disturbed by behavioral problems often reinforce their students negative behaviors.

Teachers who are prepared to meet the behavioral needs of their students project a sense of security in their classrooms. It is not that they are waiting to pounce on inappropriate behaviors but, rather, through their management style they project value on the academic process as well as on the need for order. Teachers with this "style" are perceived by students as positive. By providing a safe environment, they project their belief in the value of each student. This belief is an extremely powerful component of behavior management. The following example illustrates this point.

> Teacher X was perceived by students with conduct disorders as a "good guy." In teacher rating scales students consistently rated

him as excellent, fair, and a good teacher. There were few behavior problems in his classes, even with the conduct disordered population of the school. Researchers investigating this teacher expected to find a young or handsome person with a dynamic flair in teaching style. Instead, they found that he was average in both respects. They noted, however, the "personal style" with which he interacted with students. He leaned in the doorway between classes and really spoke to all his students, saying such things as "John, you look good today" and "Nice job on the test yesterday, Sue." Most important in these interactions was his use of the students' names. He made his interactions personal and let his students know that he genuinely cared about them.

Teachers who believe that behavior satisfies needs and represents past learning can address behavior as actions capable of change and can see their students as capable of learning new behaviors. Again, the belief that behavior management is an important component of teaching is critical to successful teaching and learning.

Teacher mindset and attitude are critical and vital factors in effecting behavior change. Teachers who view their role holistically will plan and prepare for their students' behavioral needs just as they do for their academic needs. They will accept that not all students arrive in the classroom "ready to learn" and will lay the groundwork for positive behavioral changes for their students.

The following chapters of this book provide "how-tos" for successful intervention with verbally and physically aggressive students. These techniques must be coupled with a positive mindset, however, or they will become mechanical and lose their effectiveness. Students know immediately which teachers and administrators believe in their potential. We have found that there is nothing more powerful in effecting behavior change than positive, respectful adult intervention.

▮ *DISCUSSION QUESTIONS*

1. In what ways can teachers present their expectations for classroom behavior to students so that they perceive their importance? Determine as many ways as possible that teachers can present and reinforce the need for behavioral expectations. What are some positive reinforcers for appropriate classroom behavior?

2. Ms. Aguilera is assigned to lunchroom duty in a high school. She is responsible for overseeing 100 students. What initial steps can she take to present her expectations to them? What type of monitoring should she do during lunchtime? What type of interactions with students should she initiate? Where should she choose to stand or sit during lunch?

3. Mr. Hernandez, a veteran teacher, has a new student in class who refuses to conform to his classroom expectations. At least once daily this student disrupts the class to the point that Mr. Hernandez must stop the lesson and devote 100% of his attention to this student. Mr. Hernandez has seldom had difficulty with student behavior and is firm, fair, and consistent in his teaching approach. What options might he try to improve his working relationship with this student?

CLASSROOM CLIMATE 2

*T*he teacher who builds a classroom environment based on respect and high positive expectations for students will reduce significantly the likelihood of verbal and physical aggression. Rutter, Maughan, Mortimore, and Ouston (1979) showed that the character of schools, even more than the character of the neighborhoods and families of the students, maintains and contributes to students' development of antisocial symptoms. Mayer, Butterworth, Nafpaktitis, and Sulzer-Azaroff (1983) showed that systematic training of teachers to decrease punishment and increase praise resulted in significant reductions in costs for the repair of vandalism.

Successful classrooms accentuate the strengths of the students and provide a warm, nurturing environment. The teachers are firm, fair, and friendly. How can the teacher ensure that he or she establishes such a classroom environment?

Throughout the school day, the teacher should be making positive statements to students for what they are doing appropriately. In our opinion at least 70% of a teacher's comments to students each day should be positive. These statements may be praise for completing an assignment well or perhaps a simple "thank you" for picking up a piece of paper from the floor. Everyone wants to be thanked and recognized for what they do correctly—children are certainly no exception.

Praise should be specific to the action and not global. As an example, consider the following situation. Mary has stayed in her seat throughout the lesson. If the teacher goes up to Mary and says, "Mary, you're a good girl," Mary will associate sitting in her seat with being a good person—a message that is not appropriate. More effective would be for the teacher to say, "Mary, I really appreciate your staying in your seat. Thank you." Mary will then learn the specific behavior the teacher wants to see.

We have seen many teachers use their students' names in a negative way—to call attention to them when they are doing something wrong. For example, the teacher may say, "Mary, I told you to sit in your seat." Because children like to hear their names, Mary may be happy that she got the teacher's attention. But it is much better to use Mary's name positively, saying, for example, "Mary, thanks for raising your hand."

■ *CLASSROOM EXPECTATIONS*

All classrooms should have set rules or expectations. Children need to know what is expected of them. In setting up a positive classroom climate, teachers should word expectations positively. For example:

1. Raise your hand before speaking.

2. Keep your hands to yourself.
3. Use appropriate language.
4. Stay in your seat.

Such positively worded expectations are preferable to those that focus on the negative, such as, "No talking," "No foul language," "No getting out of your seat." (See Sample Classroom Management Plan in the Appendix.)

Classroom expectations should be clear and prominently posted. High schools are notorious for providing manuals that state school rules and the consequences for breaking them. Unfortunately, most students will not read these manuals, and those who do read them will often forget their content by the end of the first week of school.

Because some students are auditory learners and others are visual learners, teachers should periodically review the posted rules. To see how well students remember the rules, some teachers conduct contests in which students are rewarded for correctly summarizing what the rules state.

In addition to posting classroom expectations, teachers must establish rewards for students who follow the rules. They may, for instance, decide to allocate a small amount of free time at the end of the day or send a positive note to the students' parents. When deciding what rewards to use, teachers must think about what is motivating to each student in the classroom. In the early days of behavior modification, teachers assumed that M & M's® were reinforcing to all students when, in fact, that was not the case. Commercial reinforcer surveys and sample reinforcement menus are now available (Cummins, 1988). Teachers must also be careful to provide the reinforcement often enough for the students. We have seen teachers offer as reinforcement a movie to be seen at the end of the month, yet primary and even many secondary students cannot delay gratification for that long. Some type of reward may need to be provided daily or weekly. Further, all physical reinforcers should be accompanied by verbal reinforcers.

From our work with children with severe behavioral problems, we have adopted the belief that one should never take good behavior for granted. Younger students enjoy being praised in front of their peers. Older students (grades six and above), who often fear being called "teacher's pets" by their peers, tend to prefer to be praised in private.

Modeling is another technique that is effective for reinforcing appropriate behavior in younger students. If fifteen students are out of their seats and talking out and two students are in their seats and being quiet, a good strategy is for the teacher to praise the students who are in their seats, saying, for example, "I like the way Mary and Bill are sitting quietly in their seats." Usually the other students will return to their seats when they observe that Mary and Bill received the teacher's attention.

At times, teachers may decide to ignore an inappropriate behavior, a technique known as *extinction*. However, two important points about extinction must be understood. First, when a behavior is ignored, it typically gets worse before it gets better because the student will test the teacher, trying to get him or her to break down and give in. Johnny may think, "I'll find Mrs. Jones's breaking point." If a teacher decides to ignore an inappropriate behavior, he or she will have to weather the storm and be prepared for the behavior to get worse before it gets better.

Second, ignoring is effective only if the teacher also reinforces and recognizes the opposite, appropriate behavior. In the following scenario, Mr. O'Reilly uses extinction appropriately and effectively with Billy, a student who is out of his seat a great deal. Mr. O'Reilly decides to ignore

Billy when he is out of his seat. Billy's out-of-seat behavior gets worse, but finally Billy sits in his seat. Mr. O'Reilly immediately says to Billy, "Thank you for getting in your seat—I certainly appreciate it." He also gives Billy special attention for being in his seat. The technique works but only if, as here, the teacher praises the child frequently when he is in his seat.

▌ CLASSROOM WORK

Appropriately planned activities can minimize the opportunity for behavioral problems. How? Students who are excited about learning and eager to do activities planned by the teacher are less likely than others to have behavioral problems. Consequently, the teacher should plan activities that are highly motivating and challenging for all students. Likewise, because students today tend to become bored easily, so the teacher should change activities frequently and provide a fast pace in the classroom. In addition, students need to see the reason behind doing the activities—the reason for learning what is being taught. Thus, the teacher should relate what is being learned to the interests of the students.

Many of today's students come to school as "passive learners." They are used to watching television and expect to be entertained by the teacher. The teacher must be a "performer," but he or she must also break the students' habit of passivity by getting them involved in the learning process. Everyone learns better by doing than being told. Children need to be actively involved in the learning process.

Too many teachers have students do busy work because it requires less planning than appropriately planned activities. However, work that is not relevant to students can result in behavioral problems, which, in turn, will result in more work for the teacher.

Also important is providing the right amount of work for the designated period of time. When students have idle time, behavioral problems will often arise. Students who have the time to get into trouble most likely will.

Although work should be challenging and exciting, if it is too difficult the students can become frustrated and in many cases will begin to act up. A personal anecdote illustrates this point. Some time ago, I was working with a teacher who was having major behavioral problems with a student in class. I asked to look at the student's most recent achievement test scores. The scores were at the third-grade level and were thought to be an accurate measure of the student's abilities. However, the teacher was giving the student work at the sixth-grade level. I suggested that the teacher reassess the level of the work given to the student. When the teacher did so and began to give the student work at a lower level, the student's behavioral problems significantly decreased.

Similarly, too much work given at one time can cause students to become frustrated and start acting up. All teachers have seen math pages containing 100 problems. Johnny, who does not like math in the first place and sees no need to learn it, often gets upset by the amount of problems assigned and usually will not even try to do the task. Like most people, Johnny feels overwhelmed when tasks build up; he wonders how he is going to get all the work done, and then he gets angry and upset.

Changes in classroom routine can also result in behavioral problems. Such changes are sometimes unavoidable—for example, on school picture days, early dismissal days, because of snow closings—but how the teacher handles the changes in classroom routine is critical. On days in which the classroom routine must be changed, the teacher should clearly outline his or her exact expectations. On school picture day, for example, students may be told that they will have so many minutes to get ready before having their picture taken, that they will be expected to wait quietly in line, and they will be given a small treat after having their picture taken if they follow the rules.

■ HANDLING DISCIPLINE PROBLEMS

In most instances of verbal aggression and other behavioral problems, teachers can, and should, attend to the problem without assistance. (Cases of physical aggression are an exception and will be discussed later.) Each time a teacher sends a student to the principal's office for a minor behavioral problem, that teacher sends a message to the student that he or she cannot handle the problem. Thus, the teacher weakens his or her authority in the eyes of the student. The characters that follow provide specific techniques that will result in better management within the classroom.

Teachers should also follow through with exactly what they say when behavioral problems occur. The teacher who tells Johnny he will have to stay after school because he did not get his work done but then remembers that she has a teacher's meeting after school that she must attend has made a threat that she cannot carry through. She therefore has weakened her position as an authority figure. She only has to do this once to send the message that she does not follow through with what she says she is going to do. Teachers should never make threats that they cannot apply.

It is impossible to change everything about a student's behavior overnight. The student's behavior did not develop overnight, and it cannot be changed that quickly either. Often progress will occur in small steps. When working with a student, the teacher should zero in on one behavior at a time, usually starting with the behavior that is most bothersome or most disruptive. Although teachers will often want to change everything about a student's behavior, we strongly recommend focusing on one behavior at a time.

Figure 2.1 presents a checklist teachers can use to assess the effectiveness of their behavioral management techniques. It provides a summary of the important points in this chapter. The more checkmarks in the yes column, the more effective one's behavior management techniques are.

■ *DISCUSSION QUESTIONS*

1. Review the rules for your school. Are they clear? Are they posted? Has the school established rewards for following the rules and specific consequences for not following the rules?
2. Think back to your classes yesterday. Which student caused you the most behavioral problems? What did he or she do that was positive? Did you recognize those behaviors?
3. Think about all of the activities you do in your classroom. Which are meaningful for your students, and which are really only busywork?
4. How many times have you sent students to the principal's office for discipline? Could you have handled those discipline problems yourself?

Yes	No	
_____	_____	1. Are the majority of statements you make during the day to each child in your class positive?
_____	_____	2. Have you stated class rules positively?
_____	_____	3. Do all students know the consequences for breaking the rules?
_____	_____	4. Do you use your students' names in a positive way?
_____	_____	5. Do you reinforce your students' behaviors rather than making general comments such as, "You're a good girl"?
_____	_____	6. Do you give students choices and encourage their decision-making skills?
_____	_____	7. Do you follow through with exactly what you say you will do?
_____	_____	8. Is the work that you give students at an appropriate level, and is it in the right amount?
_____	_____	9. Do you know what motivates each student in your classroom?
_____	_____	10. Do you encourage students to model other students' appropriate behaviors?
_____	_____	11. Do you take older students aside when you thank them for appropriate behavior?
_____	_____	12. After a blow-up or a fight, do you talk with the student about how he or she could better deal with the situation the next time it occurs?

FIGURE 2.1
A Behavior Management Checklist for Classroom Teachers
(continued)

_____	_____	13. Do you avoid verbal confrontations when a student is angry?
_____	_____	14. Do you teach your students compensating skills for dealing with anger?
_____	_____	15. Do you attempt as much as possible to resolve discipline problems in the classroom?
_____	_____	16. Do you allow students to have their own space?
_____	_____	17. Do you avoid letting the student know that he or she is getting to you?
_____	_____	18. When attempting to modify a particular student's negative behavior, do you zero in on one behavior at a time?
_____	_____	19. If you are ignoring an inappropriate behavior, do you positively reinforce for the opposite, appropriate behavior?
_____	_____	20. Do you allow students to earn privileges?

FIGURE 2.1
A Behavior Management Checklist for Classroom Teachers

■ REFERENCES

Cummins, K. (1988). *The teacher's guide to behavioral interventions.* Columbia, MO: Hawthorne.

Mayer, G. R., Butterworth, T., Nafpaktitis, M., & Sulzer-Azaroff, B. (1983). Preventing school vandalism and improving discipline: A three year study. *Journal of Applied Behavior Analysis, 16,* 355–369.

Rutter, M., Maughan, B., Mortimore, P., & Ouston, J. (1979). *Fifteen thousand hours: Secondary schools and their effects on children.* Cambridge, MA: Harvard University Press.

CLASSROOM MANAGEMENT TECHNIQUES THAT FAIL 3

Many management techniques used by teachers and administrators in today's schools simply do not work. Unfortunately, many educators continue to use unsuccessful techniques and become frustrated when they do not see a positive change in student behavior. In this chapter we review unsuccessful management techniques and discuss why they do not work. The techniques are summarized in Table 3.1.

One commonly used, ineffective technique is force. It is almost impossible to force someone to do something that he or she does not want to do. A teacher who is small in size will not be able to force a 300-pound student to do something if that student does not want to do it. And the use of force sends a poor message to students—that educators are there to bully them.

Another unsuccessful management technique, ridiculing, is not only ineffective but is also inconsistent with the belief that teachers should treat students with respect.

TABLE 3.1
Behavior Management Techniques That Fail

1. Using force
2. Ridiculing
3. Forcing students to admit lies and errors
4. Demanding confessions
5. Confronting students over issues
6. Asking students why they act out
7. Punishing students
8. Making disapproving comments
9. Comparing a student's acting-out behavior with other children's behavior
10. Yelling at students
11. Engaging in verbal battles
12. Making unrealistic threats

Source: Adapted from *Managing the Unmanageable Student* by M. Beck, T. Coleman, and D. Wineman, 1985, Lexington, MA: Ginn Press.

When a teacher tells a student, "That is the dumbest thing I have ever seen you do," the teacher is making fun of the student, harming the student's self-concept, and doing nothing to change the student's behavior except helping the student develop hostility toward the teacher or convincing the student to withdraw and refuse to do anything for the teacher.

Forcing students to admit lies and errors is also ineffective. Most children will resist letting a teacher know that they have lied or made a mistake. No one wants to admit that he or she is wrong. Instead, many students will begin to argue with the teacher.

Likewise, it is ineffective to demand a confession from a student. The teacher may have to wait a long time for the student to admit that he or she has done something wrong. Many times the student will be convinced that he or she has not done anything wrong.

Confrontational techniques not only are ineffective but usually result in the student becoming angry and hostile. By being confrontational, the teacher is daring the student to become aggressive.

Another common, misguided approach used by educators is to ask the student why he or she did something. Consider the scenario of Johnny pulling Mary's hair. If the teacher asks Johnny why he pulled Mary's hair, he will (1) not respond, (2) make up an answer he thinks the teacher wants to hear, or (3) tell the teacher the real reason. But, in any case, what has been accomplished? I am reminded of the time the police called to report that the tape player one of my students had brought to school was stolen. I called the student into my office and asked why he took the tape player. His answer was: "Because I wanted it." The answer was logical, but where did it get me? I still had to deal with the fact that he had stolen a tape player.

Punishment is another frequently used, unsuccessful management technique. In the schools it may take the form of reprimands, poor grades, corporal punishment (paddling), scolding, or ridicule. Although punishment may get rid of an unwanted behavior quickly, it does not result in a long-lasting positive change in behavior. B. F. Skinner said it well in 1938: "The use of punishment is counterproductive because it causes the learner to pay more attention to the punishment than to the material to be learned" (cited in Beck, Coleman, & Wineman, 1985).

Fortunately, more states each year are banning the use

of corporal punishment because it teaches that it is okay for adults to hit children. Teachers must send the opposite message—that violence is not acceptable. One way they can do so is by modeling, that is, by not using violence themselves.

Research has shown that making disapproving comments to a student is also ineffective. It simply calls attention to the inappropriate behavior. Beck et al. (1985) found that students' disruptive behavior increased when the number of disapproving remarks made by a teacher was tripled.

Comparing the acting-out behavior of one student with other's inappropriate behavior is also ineffective. Telling Johnny, " I had your brother in school and he was a problem and you act just like him," sends Johnny the message that he is not important. Students live up to teachers' expectations; if Johnny's teacher expects him to act like his brother and verbalizes that expectation to Johnny, chances are he will act like his brother.

Similarly, yelling at students is ineffective and unproductive yet all too common in U.S. schools. A visitor walking down the hall of a school will often hear an upset teacher yelling at his or her students. Teachers and students raise their voices to get attention or to express anger. Unfortunately, the person being yelled at typically responds by becoming louder too, and before long both are engaged in a shouting match with neither listening to the other person. Yelling also tends to make the person being yelled at feel defensive. The same result occurs: That person becomes angry and raises his or her voice. Often that is exactly what the yeller wants—to see the yellee get upset.

Other types of verbal battles also are useless. When a student is upset with the teacher, he or she will want to argue. The worst thing the teacher can do is take up the challenge. Engaging in an argument simply feeds the already inappropriate situation. Further, when a student is arguing and has lost control, he or she will not be able to listen to reason. Arguing would be futile.

Finally, as previously mentioned, many teachers resort to making unrealistic threats they cannot implement. Not only is this technique ineffective, but it damages the teacher's authority. When a teacher makes a comment to a student like, "That's it, you have lost recess for the rest of the year," and then reneges, realizing the punishment was too harsh, the teacher weakens his or her authority in the student's eyes. The message the teacher sends is loud and clear; I may not always do what I say I will do. The student learns that the teacher cannot be trusted. In a positive classroom climate, the student must know that the teacher's word is good.

The management techniques discussed in this chapter, although commonly used by educators, do not work. We strongly recommend that they not be used. The behavior management techniques described in the rest of this book are much more effective and productive.

▌ DISCUSSION QUESTIONS

1. Think back to your classes yesterday. How many of the management techniques discussed in this chapter were used?
2. The last time someone yelled at you, how did you handle it? Was your method effective?
3. How many times in a day do you use punishment as a classroom management technique? What types of punishment do you use?

▮ *REFERENCES*

Beck, M., Coleman, T., & Wineman, D. (1985). *Managing the unmanageable student.* Lexington, MA Ginn Press.

PRACTICAL TIPS FOR SUCCESSFUL BEHAVIOR MANAGEMENT 4

The practical tips for successful behavior management given in this chapter are actually the underpinnings of all good teaching practices. When teachers employ these strategies in their daily contacts with students, their interactions generally have positive and productive outcomes. When thinking about these strategies, which are summarized below, one must keep in mind that respect for others is the cornerstone of every quality intervention. Because teachers are at all times role models for their students, they must consistently show respect as they carry out any behavior management strategy.

TIPS FOR SUCCESSFUL BEHAVIOR MANAGEMENT

1. Build rapport
2. Accent the positive
3. Censure pupils in private

4. Adhere to the maxim "Nothing succeeds like success"
5. Make lessons motivating
6. Do not take a student's misbehavior personally
7. Never force an issue with a difficult student in front of the class
8. Remember that every consequence not carried out weakens a teacher's status
9. Find out what a student does well and build on it
10. Avoid sarcasm
11. Do not label students as "bad" or "sneaky"
12. Help the class formulate class rules; strive for self-discipline; set high standards
13. Do not look for miracles overnight
14. Be consistent
15. Keep calm
16. Praise the class as a group and as individuals
17. Be aware that prevention is better than punishment
18. Deal with problems immediately
19. Ensure that student's take responsibility for their actions
20. Inform parents of positives as well as problems
21. Retain a good sense of humor

▌ *BUILDING RAPPORT*

In acts as simple as greeting a student by name, a teacher can begin to establish rapport with a student. Finding something the student does well and taking time to talk with the student about it builds further rapport. Basically, taking a genuine interest in students provides the groundwork for good rapport.

We have placed the establishment of rapport first in this list of practical tips because a positive relationship with a student is vital for effective behavioral intervention. When a student knows that a teacher has taken the time to genuinely talk with, encourage, or compliment him or her, the student is far more likely to listen to and follow the teacher's requests for compliance and expectations of appropriate behavior.

ACCENT THE POSITIVE

Teachers should never miss an opportunity to honestly accent the positive. In our opinion, at least 70% of the comments teachers give students each day should be positive. With some students, providing such a large amount of positive feedback may seem nearly impossible. However, accenting the positive fills two important roles: It greatly contributes to building rapport, and it helps build the students' self-esteem.

Students frequently use misbehavior to relieve pressure when they feel insecure. Thus, every opportunity teachers have to build their students' self-esteem is an opportunity to reduce inappropriate behavior.

CENSURE PUPILS IN PRIVATE

No one appreciates being disciplined in front of his or her peers. It is out of respect for students that we advocate censuring them privately. Teachers can pull students aside or ask them to stay after class to discuss concerns, or they can speak to students in a quiet hall area or during a study hall time. It is especially important that teachers talk with students at the first sign of behavior problems rather than waiting until problems escalate.

When discussing concerns with students, teachers should make sure the students completely understand the classroom expectations and should offer them the opportunity to make the necessary changes in the classroom. It is important to ask probing questions about the situation and really listen, without interrupting, to the students' responses. Some effective questions are: "Is there something about the material you are having problems with?" "Is there any part of the course work that I can assist with?" "What areas of the subject matter do you enjoy the most?" "Is there a particular part of the homework that gives you difficulty?" "Is there a student you would rather sit beside?" Teachers should avoid questions such as, "Why are you doing (this)?" and "Why can't you get along with Sue?" These questions only lead students down the path of blame and idle responses.

The conversation should be kept focused on the task or behavior that needs to be modified and positive ways of correcting the problem. The teacher should be brief, quickly getting to the point and not repeating statements. Just enough should be said to show concern and a willingness to cooperatively work out any problem. A good strategy is to begin the conversation by directly stating the concern or problem and to end it by reminding the student of a situation in which he or she acted appropriately.

▊ ADHERE TO THE MAXIM "NOTHING SUCCEEDS LIKE SUCCESS"

Students who have had a history of behavioral difficulties in school tend to view each new class or teacher as an experience that will further verify that school is negative and that they are failures in the school setting. Such students often set up the teacher or situation in a way that will continue the pattern of failure. Circumventing this routine—by developing projects, activities, tasks, cooperative learning experiences, and assignments that will build self-confidence—requires planning on the part of the teacher. However, the result will be well worth the effort.

One suggestion is to give students choices when assigning projects, homework, or activities. Doing so gives them some control and allows them to choose options that appeal to their strongest learning modality. Another suggestion is to give students the opportunity to improve their grades on assignments by correcting or revising their work. (Usually this option applies only to assignments and not to tests.) Because revision is not mandatory, students who are satisfied with their grades can do nothing while others can take advantage of the opportunity to improve their work and learn from their mistakes. This option places more work on the teacher, but, more important, it emphasizes learning and the teacher's belief in the value of what is being taught.

No matter what structure the classwork has, it is important to compliment every student who does well, even those who seem to disregard the compliment. Teachers should never leave any deserving student out when complimenting success or accomplishment.

▮ MAKE LESSONS MOTIVATING

Students respond to instructors who are interested in the learning process and excited about the material they teach. Lessons should not involve stale repetition. In each class the subject matter can be related to the world of the students. Academics without relevance to the students' world leads to boredom, which leads to disruptive behavior.

Teachers who believe in the need to relate academics

to the students' world incorporate extended activities, hands-on learning, cooperative tasks, experimental learning activities, life skill activities, and variety into their lessons and use motivational strategies in their classes. Their highly interactive approach to teaching is similar to that used in "gifted" programs. Teachers who make the subject matter relevant and interesting face fewer behavior problems.

▌ *DO NOT TAKE A STUDENT'S MISBEHAVIOR PERSONALLY*

One of the biggest challenges faced by teachers is to not take students' misbehavior and verbal comments personally. However, it is critical that teachers follow this advice. Students who fling verbal comments, insults, slurs, and threats at the teacher are attempting to get a reaction. They are trying to upset the teacher. They are looking for the red face, the dramatic or rash statements and actions, the smart reply or put-down. They may hope to be kicked out of class. Such students win victories when the teacher reacts to their comments in a way that lets them and their classmates know that the teacher is hurt or angry.

All teachers have overheard students making comments like, "You should have seen (or heard) Mr. Smith when James told him that he was a big fat...!" By letting James know that his comment was taken personally, Mr. Smith gave control to James and lost respect. Admittedly, it can be very difficult to keep personal feelings out of the situation, but a good rule of thumb is to focus on the inappropriate behavior, rather than the student's comment, and calmly state that it is not acceptable behavior in the classroom. The teacher can then state the classroom or school rules that apply to the behavior. By responding in this manner, the teacher keeps the intervention focused on the misbehavior, maintains a professional attitude, and does not allow the situation to escalate into a verbal battle.

▎ *NEVER FORCE AN ISSUE WITH A DIFFICULT STUDENT IN FRONT OF THE CLASS*

As mentioned in Chapter 3, force is a strategy that is sure to fail when intervening with a verbally or physically aggressive student. When a teacher forces an issue with such a student in front of the class, he or she creates a situation that is dangerous to the emotional well-being of the student, the teacher, and the others in the class. The student will feel the need to "save face" because the teacher has taken the position of "You will do this, and I will make you do it." Students in this type of scenario have three options: (1) complying; (2) arguing and fighting the teacher's power move; and (3) arguing and trying to pull others from the class into the argument.

Students who choose compliance with the teacher will understandably feel anger at being treated in such a manner in front of their peers. This situation can breed lasting contempt for the teacher. Others in the classroom will also be affected; many will feel personally offended by the teacher's position. By using force, the teacher may set up long-lasting feelings of mistrust in the students.

With the second option, the argumentative student takes control. The teacher must either continue to force the issue or back down, neither of which is a positive option. If the teacher does not back down, a verbal battle ensues, which stresses the entire class. Often the mere feat of engaging a teacher in a verbal battle is a victory for the aggressive student.

Highly manipulative students often will employ the third option. By pulling others into the argument, they make it more difficult for the teacher to regain control of the group. In this no-win situation the entire class is stressed, and often the teacher needs help regaining control of the situation.

None of these options results in a desirable outcome. Teachers would do well to heed the advice of never forcing an issue with a difficult student in front of the class.

▌ *REMEMBER THAT EVERY CONSEQUENCE NOT CARRIED OUT WEAKENS A TEACHER'S STATUS*

Teachers who follow through with their statements concerning discipline or any other commitment show a consistency that students can count on. Students feel secure knowing that the teacher will always follow through with his or her commitments. Conversely, teachers who do not follow through with their statements create an insecure environment. Students cannot rely on them for consistency. Aggressive or defiant students often will misbehave because they know the teacher may not enforce the consequence for their inappropriate behavior. The chance that the teacher will not follow through is enough enticement for some students to try to get away with aggression or misbehavior.

Teachers who do not follow through with their statements, especially regarding consequences for misbehavior, leave themselves open to the accusation that they do not treat all students fairly, which can result in major problems in classroom management. Disruptive students, like all other students, want fair treatment. It is tempting at times to overlook a problem or not follow through with the consequences due to the time and effort needed for intervention. However, whenever teachers do not follow through with a stated consequence they weaken their ability to maintain an orderly classroom.

Teachers must be careful not to make extreme statements regarding consequences for misbehavior. Such statements may be impossible to carry through. All consequences must be realistic and enforceable.

The importance of planning for students' misbehavior and having a system in place for dealing with it cannot be overstated. A teacher who plans ahead for inappropriate behavior has thought out reasonable and enforceable consequences and has at hand a plan of action for dealing with disruptions. As part of the plan the teacher clearly explains to students his or her behavioral expectations as well as the consequences related to inappropriate behaviors. All explanations and actions of the teacher are based on the importance of maintaining a safe, orderly learning environment for all students.

By having a plan of action in place, the teacher is better able to remove him- or herself from highly charged emotional conflicts. The teacher does not randomly hand out consequences for misbehavior. Consistency is in place, and fairness follows. The teacher can, by relying on his or her plan of action, carry out consequences in a firm and fair manner.

■ *FIND OUT WHAT A STUDENT DOES WELL AND BUILD ON IT*

We believe that all students genuinely want to be accepted. However, students with a history of school failure or behavior problems often see themselves as inadequate in the school setting and compensate by confirming this inadequacy with each teacher through misbehavior that leads to discipline. One way to counteract their feelings of low self-esteem is for the teacher to find common grounds of interest with these students and engage them in conversation focused on these areas. Activities and assignments can be developed that further draw on the strength of their interests.

Although teachers have busy schedules, we cannot overstress the importance of taking the time for casual conversation with students about their interests. Simply giving a student a few minutes of undivided positive attention can be a real boost. Even if a student seems distant at first, the teacher should not stop the interaction. Students who have experienced limited positive teacher relationships will likely be wary of staff who give them attention. Developing a trusting relationship takes time. For the student who is hesitant, the teacher may want to start with a simple casual conversation at the end of class or during hall time. Just saying hello to the student is a good beginning.

■ *AVOID SARCASM*

Sarcastic statements are seen by students, and others, as verbal put-downs. Aggressive students may see this type of interaction as a challenge. Such students will usually make a reply to "save face." It is very difficult for the aggressive student to let sarcasm pass without response.

Our advice is for teachers to avoid sarcasm and keep interactions with students positive and productive. By maintaining respectful interactions with students, teachers are modeling the behaviors that they want students to display in the classroom.

▌ *DO NOT LABEL STUDENTS AS "BAD" OR "SNEAKY"*

Students have a way of living up or down to the labels put on them. Although teachers may be only half serious when they label students as "Trouble" or "Big mouth," aggressive students, those with low self-esteem, and those looking for an avenue through which they will be accepted may see such labels as a means of identification. Many will live up to the behavior the label implies to maintain status.

If teachers or staff want to give a label, a positive label is far better than a negative one. A number of cases have been brought to our attention of staff actually reducing negative behaviors with positive labels. By picking up on an appropriate behavior, making a comment (label) about that behavior, and reinforcing the behavior, staff can influence positive change. For example, consider the case of Tom:

As a result of extremely impoverished living conditions, Tom never bathed or attended to personal hygiene before school. His clothes were never laundered. Tom's disposition matched his appearance: He was grouchy, angry, and frequently swore as he got off the bus.

Staff would greet him as he got off the bus, but his response for months was to scowl and look away or mumble under his breath. Finally, after several months of greeting Tom, a staff member got a small smile from him. From that time on she began to call him "Smiley." Tom began to accept the label, and each morning he would smile as she addressed him as Smiley.

Over time, Tom began to smile at others during the day. All of the staff members commented about his great smile. Something as simple as a positive label helped Tom break out of the pervasive negative mood that kept him from positive social contact.

▌*HELP THE CLASS FORMULATE CLASS RULES; STRIVE FOR SELF-DISCIPLINE; SET HIGH STANDARDS*

A primary goal for teachers when working with students who frequently exhibit aggressive behaviors is to assist them in learning self-discipline and controlling their aggressive impulsive behaviors. Teachers who approach their students' aggression from an instructional standpoint will allow these students to help formulate the class rules and consequences for misbehavior. By taking part in this procedure, the students learn the reasons for the rules and the need for an equitable consequence system.

We have found that students respond with the most acceptance to rules and consequences when they help establish them. Most students who participate in some portion of establishing class rules or expectations feel a personal responsibility to live up to the plan.

The class meeting approach can be used to provide a forum for student input. We are not suggesting that students set all classroom rules and consequences. Rather, we recommend that teachers initially develop an overall plan for behavior management in the classroom that gives basic expectations, sets limits, and establishes overall consequences. Then, at the beginning of the school year, the teacher can present the plan to the class and lead an open discussion on the need for rules and on the specific rules and their consequences. Rules can be modified, added, or deleted based on this discussion.

The class meeting can become a forum for discussion throughout the school year. Meetings can occur daily or on a periodic schedule. During the first week of school the teacher should outline the method of participation in the class meeting. Simple guidelines can be set up that are appropriate not only for class meetings but also for academic class participation. The following is one example:

CLASS MEETING GUIDELINES

1. Each person is entitled to his or her opinion.
2. Use "I" statements to express feelings.
3. Make eye contact when speaking.
4. Put no one down.
5. Only one person speaks at a time; everyone has the right to be heard.
6. Use active listening.

At class meetings students can voice their opinions; they have an opportunity to be heard and to listen to others. The discussions should not solely focus on class rules, however. Class meetings can and should be used for planning special events and celebrations, discussing current events, talking about student and staff concerns, and planning community or school activities. The class meeting can also be used as a setting for teaching social skills.

The teacher's role at the class meeting is one of a moderator as well as a participant. Although the teacher can give his or her opinion, group decisions should be made through a democratic voting process. As group facilitator, the teacher ensures that the decisions to be made by the group are appropriate for student determination. As with any system, some decisions remain the responsibility of the teacher.

Once the class meeting framework and class rules are in place, class meetings can be used to discuss rule infractions that do not clearly fall into the broad guidelines of the structure. Consider the following experience, which occurred when I instituted class meetings in a classroom of seven students with severe behavioral disorders.

> Sam was angry with a floating teacher's assistant who had given him a zero on his point sheet because he yelled at her during his English tutoring time. Earlier, the teacher's assistant had offered to pay Sam to do some decorative woodworking for her. After he was given the zero, Sam gouged the wood project with an ink pen, writing: "Oops, That's a zero, sorry."
>
> The teacher's assistant brought the issue of property damage before the group at the next class meeting. She explained that one student in the class had damaged her property and asked the group to determine how this situation should be handled.
>
> The students were asked to express what they would want and how they would feel if the student had damaged their property. They expressed several opinions, including doing nothing if the cost of the damage was less than fifty cents and removing all of the student's classroom privileges until the damage was repaid. After much discussion the group unanimously determined that the student should repay, regardless of the amount, the cost of the damage and apologize to the teacher's assistant. All of the student's classroom privileges would be denied until these conditions were met. Each person at the meeting, including the teacher and the teacher's assistant, voted in favor.
>
> Sam, who was a master at denying, arguing, and manipulating, said nothing. After two days without privileges, he paid the cost of the damage and apologized. There were no other incidents of property damage after the class meeting.

This example illustrates the value of student input into classroom planning. Direct involvement leads to self-discipline. Although this strategy works best in self-contained classes, it can be successful in most settings in which students meet on a consistent basis.

▐ *DO NOT LOOK FOR MIRACLES OVERNIGHT*

Behavior change takes time. When implementing a new intervention for behavior change with any student, teachers must allow adequate time for the intervention to be effective (Walker & Shea, 1984). Students, especially those who are aggressive and have used that aggression successfully for a significant amount of time, may be resistant to new interventions. Their behavior at the onset of the intervention will often become worse as they test the teacher's ability to remain calm and consistent. As mentioned in Chapter 1, misbehavior often satisfies a need, and the thought of changing that behavior is threatening. For students with significant behavior problems, the intervention must incorporate teaching alternative, appropriate behaviors to help the students meet their needs.

Teachers should carry out new interventions for at least three weeks before assessing their impact. During that time, the teacher should continually praise and reinforce the student's positive behaviors and enforce the consequences for inappropriate behaviors. The most important message the teacher can give to the student is that he or she believes in the student's ability to behave appropriately.

With some students, especially those with behavioral disorders, the length of time for an intervention to have an impact can be much longer than three weeks. Noticeable change may take months.

▐ *BE CONSISTENT*

Inconsistency between what a teacher says and what he or she does is one of the most damaging influences on positive behavior intervention. Students who are aggressive or disruptive often behave inappropriately with teachers who are inconsistent in their approach to behavior management because they know there is always the chance that such teachers will not enforce the consequences. Some students truly get a thrill out of the thought that there may not be a consequence for their actions.

Although it is tempting to sometimes overlook misbehavior, nearly every piece of literature regarding behavioral intervention strategies discusses the need for consistency. Consistency not only discourages misbehavior but also provides security for students. By maintaining a dispassionate sense of fairness through consistent enforcement of classroom and school rules, the teacher creates a safe environment that fosters respect. In this environment, the teacher enforces the rules and consequences fairly with all students, never singling out a particular student or group.

■ *KEEP CALM*

As mentioned in earlier chapters, using a calm, low voice is vital to successful behavioral intervention. In addition, the teacher must maintain his or her poise. When a student becomes highly aggressive verbally, a good strategy is for the teacher to briefly restate, using behavior specific dialogue (Johns, Carr, & Hoots, in press), the classroom expectation the student should be following at that moment. (See Chapter 7.) This type of dialogue allows the student and the teacher time to think and respond appropriately. It also prevents excessive talk—dialogue that is nonproductive in resolving the situation. If the student tries to bring up past incidents or the situations of others to sidetrack the issue, the teacher should directly state that he or she is willing to talk only about the current situation. Briefly restating the classroom expectation takes the burden of being the "bad guy" off the teacher, as he or she is simply enforcing a preestablished expectation firmly and fairly. It also eliminates many opportunities for the student to argue with the teacher.

We believe that teachers should make very clear to students that they will not argue with them. Whenever a student begins arguing in an accusatory, out-of-control manner, the teacher should simply say, "I'll talk with you when you are calm." The teacher should then step to the side and wait a few seconds. If the student calms down, the teacher can begin the conversation again. However, if the student's anger escalates, the teacher should repeat his or her statement about waiting until the student is calm and should then wait a few more seconds before trying the conversation again. This simple technique helps keep both the student and the teacher poised and calm.

Acting calmly, even when one does not feel calm, will be a tension reducer to not only the disruptive student but to the others in the class as well. If all of the students in the class know that the teacher is at all times ready to deal with disruptive situations, the onlooking students will be less likely to join in the inappropriate behavior. Remember, to maintain poise, the teacher should use a low, calm voice, refrain from arguing with students, use behavior specific dialogue, and state the applicable, preestablished classroom expectation and consequence.

A student's disruptive behavior can be looked at as an opportunity for modeling socially acceptable behavior. Each time a teacher responds to disruptive behavior, calmly, he or she is modeling a positive alternative to verbal or physical aggression.

▮ *PRAISE THE CLASS AS A GROUP AND AS INDIVIDUALS*

Students need and deserve praise for demonstrating appropriate behaviors, quality academic performance, and appropriate social skills. Praise should be given immediately and should be stated with specific reasons for the recognition. If the reasons for the praise are not stated, the praise may not have meaning for the student.

Teachers often give praise to individuals, but recognizing the group as a whole is also important. Group praise highlights the peer interactions that are necessary for cohesive group behaviors. Students with behavior problems often do not perceive themselves as being a part of the group. However, when a teacher gives both positive individual and positive group reinforcement, even these students may begin to feel a sense of group belonging.

With the increasing concern of gang involvement, this issue becomes critically important. Youth involved in gangs consistently report that they turned to gangs because they offered a sense of belonging that they did not get from home or school (Goldstein & Huff, 1993). It is vital that teachers provide opportunities for students to feel involved in the class that they reward positive involvement with genuine encouragement and praise.

▮ *BE AWARE THAT PREVENTION IS BETTER THAN PUNISHMENT*

Good behavior management begins with anticipating the types of behavior problems likely to occur in any group. Teachers who develop a plan of action have at hand the means to react effectively to reduce the negative effects of misbehavior on the offending student and the class.

Although teachers must state and enforce consequences for inappropriate behavior, guiding student behavior toward self-discipline is even more important. Nighswander (1988) indicated that teachers who preplan and organize their classrooms and interventions can prevent much misconduct.

▌ DEAL WITH PROBLEMS IMMEDIATELY

Students are more likely to engage in misbehavior when they know that their teacher may not deal with their misbehavior immediately. When the consequence is delayed, or nonexistent, the student feels that he or she is in control.

In addition, consequences that are delayed are often too removed from the problem behavior to effectively bring about positive change. We recommend immediate action at the first sign of misbehavior. Early interventions can be unobtrusive, such as moving closer in proximity to the student, making eye contact, using a gesture or cue that indicates that the student should stop what he or she is doing, and making a general reminder to the class of the on-task behavior. Interventions that can be used if the behavior persists despite unobtrusive interventions, include reminding the class of the appropriate rule, pausing until the misbehavior stops, directly appealing to the misbehaving student using behavior specific dialogue, and, as a last resort, removing the misbehaving student from the situation.

▌ ENSURE THAT STUDENTS TAKE RESPONSIBILITY FOR THEIR ACTIONS

Behavior management begins with the student taking responsibility for his or her actions. Teachers who have developed plans of action for misbehavior, posted and reviewed with students the classroom expectations and consequences, demonstrated firm, fair, and consistent interventions, and given praise fairly usually have no problem calmly allowing students to be responsible for their actions.

Students should not be allowed to blame others when they misbehave. Behavior specific dialogue, as described in Chapter 7, clearly places the responsibility for behavior choice on the student. The teacher uses statements such as, "It's your choice. Make a good decision for yourself."

When students realize that they will be held responsible for their actions, they will begin to accept responsibility. They will begin to think before they act and will make changes in their behavior. In doing so, they will show true self-discipline.

■ *INFORM PARENTS OF POSITIVES AS WELL AS PROBLEMS*

Research has shown that those students with supportive, involved parents are the most successful in school (Mendler, 1992). Finding areas in which to praise successful students is easy; the harder thing for teachers is finding the time to let parents know the positive things about their children. Unfortunately, the parents of students who have difficulty controlling aggression probably hear few positive teacher comments. Teachers should look for areas in which they can genuinely praise these students. Contact with parents should not be limited to conversations about problems.

■ *RETAIN A GOOD SENSE OF HUMOR*

The final practical tip for successful behavior management is to maintain a good sense of humor. Without the ability to laugh at some of the situations they encounter, many teachers would not be able to continue teaching. We do not mean laughing at students but with students. On days when things go wrong or when funny incidents occur, laughing with students lets them know their teacher is human. Sharing the humor in everyday occurrences is an important part of the rapport necessary for quality teaching.

▮ *DISCUSSION QUESTIONS*

1. Mr. Matthews has a student who never speaks in his class. What are five ways in which he could begin to develop rapport with that student?

2. The hall monitor reports to Ms. Ishikawa that Jim, a student in her class, has been intimidating the other students in the hall almost every day. He cannot get Jim to stop this behavior. He asks Ms. Ishikawa to bring this topic up at her next class meeting. What questions should she ask of the group? Should she invite the hall monitor to bring up the topic? What type of consequences would be appropriate? Should she speak with Jim?

3. Almost every day several students arrive unprepared for Mrs. Blair's class. They do not bring paper, pencils, or their textbooks. Mrs. Blair knows they have the supplies; they just do not bring them. One of her class rules is that students should come to class prepared. What can she do to stop this misbehavior? Consider rule review; consequences; class meeting; praising the class as a whole and as individuals; immediacy of dealing with the problem; censuring pupils.

4. Mr. Lightfoot knows that Tom often argues with other

students and with staff. Tom will be in Mr. Lightfoot's class this year. How can Mr. Lightfoot prevent Tom's arguing from disrupting the classroom? How should he respond to Tom's arguing? If Tom persists in arguing, what types of consequences can Mr. Lightfoot impose to reduce this problem?

▌ *REFERENCES*

Goldstein, A. P., & Huff, C. R. (1993). *The gang intervention handbook*. Champaign, IL: Research Press.

Johns, B., Carr, V., & Hoots, C. (in press). *Reduction of school violence: Alternatives to suspension*. Horsham, PA: LRP Publications.

Mendler, A. (1992). *How to achieve discipline with dignity in the classroom*. Bloomington, IN: National Educational Service.

Nighswander, J. (1988). *Tips for teachers—managing the effective classroom*. Springfield: Illinois State Board of Education.

Walker, J. E., & Shea, T. M. (1984). *Behavior management: A practical approach for educators*. St. Louis: Times Mirror/Mosby College Publishing.

UNDERSTANDING AGGRESSION 5

Aggression is a symptom of high-level frustration. The teacher who is aware of the stages of frustration (Table 5.1) can usually intervene before a student's frustration turns into aggression. Although some students, especially those with severe behavior disorders, may show few if any symptoms before a blow, most exhibit symptoms of lower-level frustration. Each stage of frustration is discussed in this chapter, and interventions are described that can assist in reducing frustration and keeping the student productive in the classroom. Included in the chapter are brief discussions of verbal aggression, physical aggression, and therapeutic communication; these topics are covered in depth in subsequent chapters.

■ FIRST-STAGE FRUSTRATION

When in the first stage of frustration with schoolwork—anxiety—students usually exhibit nonverbal cues. They often sigh, put their pencils down and stare at the text, put their heads down on their desks, or hold their head in their

TABLE 5.1
Understanding Frustration (continued)

STUDENT SYMPTOMS	TEACHER INTERVENTIONS
Anxiety Stage	**Support**
Sighs	Active listening
Puts head down	Nonjudgmental talk
Holds head in hands	Empathetic talk
Second-Stage Stress	**Interactive Support**
Taps pencil	Proximity control
Wads up paper	Hurdle help
Rips paper or breaks pencil lead when writing	Interest boosting
	Supportive assistance on assignment
Defensiveness or Verbal Aggression	**Set Clear Limits**
Slams book or fist	Brief statement of rule reminders
Says, "You can't teach!" or "I won't do this, you can't make me!"	Antiseptic bouncing
	Support through routines
Yells or argues with teacher or other student	Behavior specific dialogue
	Conflict resolution
Physical Aggression	**Physical Intervention**
Throws chair or desk	Behavior specific dialogue
Makes threatening stance toward teacher	Give choices
	Review consequences
Intimidates or threatens other students	Allow student to be responsible for his or her choice
Behaves injuriously to self or others	Call team to remove or escort student to time-out area
	Physical holding

TABLE 5.1
Understanding Frustration

Tension Reduction/Regaining Self-Control Before Returning to Class	Therapeutic Communication
Student may cry or release tension through verbal venting	Allow time for student to calm down
	Never leave student alone
	Life space interview
	Review incident
	Plan alternative behavior
	Plan for return to class
	End with positive attitude

Some of these items were described in *Managing the Unmanageable Student* by M. Beck, T. Coleman, and D. Wineman, 1985, Lexington, MA: Ginn Press.

hands. The nonverbal message to the teacher is, "Help!"

When students begin to exhibit these symptoms, teachers should give them a few more minutes to try to do the work on their own. However, if the symptoms continue, teacher intervention is warranted.

An effective strategy is active listening. The teacher can ask the student to explain his or her dilemma. As the student explains the problem, the teacher should acknowledge and give positive reinforcement for each part of work or explanation that is correct. The teacher should listen for the cause of the anxiety. Some students are simply afraid of new work; others may be trying to get the teacher's attention; some may be totally confused by the assignment.

When talking with the student, the teacher should be empathetic. This strategy is illustrated in the following interaction between a teacher and a student struggling with fractions:

> Georgia is having a hard time reducing improper fractions. She has not raised her hand for help but has erased five times and now has put her head down. The teacher walks to Georgia's desk and says, "Fractions can be difficult, right Georgia? What seems to be giving you the biggest problem?" As Georgia describes her inability to understand the reduction process, the teacher finds a way to relate the process to one Georgia is familiar with. "You know," the teacher says, "these improper fractions are actually division problems, and you are very good at division. If I do the first problem with you, I think you will see the process." After they do one problem together, the teacher asks Georgia to do the next four problems. The teacher says she will check in with Georgia when she has finished those problems to see if she has done them correctly.

During the interaction the teacher was empathetic; she did not minimize the student's concern over the task. She related the task to something with which the student felt competent. Finally, she provided a means of follow-up support by saying she would return after the student completed four problems to check on the accuracy of the student's work.

A mistake teachers frequently make is being judgmental about the difficulty of the work or problem area. It does not help to say, "This is really easy. You can do this!" The student is feeling just the opposite; comments about how easy the work is will only lead to feelings of greater inadequacy and frustration.

■ *SECOND-STAGE FRUSTRATION*

The second stage of frustration is increased stress. Some students show their irritation with an assignment by tapping their pencils. Some wad up their paper and then unwad it and try to write over their first attempts. Others hold their pencils in a "death grip" and press on the paper so hard that they tear the paper as they write or break the lead of the pencil. The student is highly stressed with the work but does not voluntarily express his or her frustration in words. Intervention may call for physically moving closer to the student, known as *proximity control* (Beck, Coleman, & Wineman, 1985).

Rather than focusing on the torn paper or broken pencil lead, the teacher should concentrate on the assignment. The ripped paper and broken lead have not interfered with any other student's learning, and no harm has been inflicted on anyone. It is best to ignore the pencil and paper and focus on the task. The teacher should check the student's paper and comment on the correct items. Such comments should bring some relief to the student. Then the teacher can work through a problem or two with the student to see where he or she is losing hold of the process. After guiding the student through one or two additional problems, the teacher can have the student complete several more without help. If a student is too tense to receive help, the teacher should say he or she will be glad to help when the student is ready.

▮ *THIRD-STAGE FRUSTRATION*

In the first and second stages of frustration, the student contains his or her feelings. The class is seldom disrupted. The casual interventions that have been described generally work well. For third-stage frustration, however, manifested by defensiveness and verbal aggression, the intervention has to be less casual and more direct. Students in the third stage often show their frustration by slamming their fists on the desk, yelling out at the teacher, or shoving a book off their desk. The defensive and verbally aggressive student is interfering with the learning climate.

At this time the teacher needs to briefly restate the appropriate class expectation, saying, for example, We do not yell in the classroom. The teacher may also state the consequence of the action. If the rule reminder stops the yelling, the teacher should let the student know that help will be available when he or she asks appropriately.

Among the expectations that teachers and student develop should be the procedure for students to follow when requesting help. Most teachers ask students to raise their hands; others have students use a signal or card on their desk to indicate that they would like help. Even students who have yelled out inappropriately should be expected to follow the class rule for getting help.

If a student persists in yelling, the teacher should employ behavior specific dialogue, as outlined in Chapter 7. With this type of dialogue the teacher gives a brief directive, allows five seconds for response, and, if necessary, repeats the directive. If it is not followed, the consequence is imposed. An appropriate consequence is to remove the student to a time-out area, thereby allowing the class to continue. Time-out should be an area in which students can regain control. After the student in time-out is quiet for five minutes, he or she should return to class.

Beck et al. (1985) suggest another strategy for intervention with defensive students, something they call antiseptic bouncing. The student is given a chore, such as delivering a note to the secretary's office, to allow a temporary break from the task at hand. Beck et al. found that the change in activity was sometimes sufficient for draining off the student's frustration so that the student could begin the task anew upon return.

When a student's defensiveness or verbal aggression is not related to school but to another student, the most effective intervention is usually conflict resolution (Johns, Carr, & Hoots, in press). The students involved in the dispute state their perceptions and feelings regarding the conflict. A mediator, often the teacher, remains neutral but guides the students through steps of active listening, problem analyzing, cooperative decision-making, and dispute settlements. The terms of the agreement are determined by the disputants. In some schools students can request conflict resolution; in others it is mandatory.

From our experience, conflict resolution is an excellent intervention technique for all students, including those with severe behavioral disorders. The conflict resolution process teaches students a format for resolving conflict and encourages open communication. Teachers are urged to review the instructional material created by Schrumpf (1991). Schrumpf"'s conflict resolution procedure is well designed and can be easily implemented in any school setting.

■ FOURTH-STAGE FRUSTRATION

When frustration moves into stage four, physical aggression, the teacher must be prepared to intervene in a way that ensures the safety of everyone in the classroom. If a student throws over his or her desk, the teacher should immediately, using behavior specific dialogue, request that the student go to the time-out room or area. Students should know that they can walk to the time-out room on their own but that the crisis response team will be called to escort them if they refuse to cooperate.

We recommend that all schools train a team of at last four staff members to be available to escort a student who is physically aggressive out of the classroom to an area of safety. The team should be trained in a form of safe physical restraint.

All schools should have in place a procedure for signaling the team in the event that a student attacks another student or staff member. The procedure may involve sending a student to the office or to another classroom for assistance or signaling through an intercom system. The teacher needs to stay with student(s) in conflict and do all that is possible to verbally stop the conflict and protect the other students in the classroom. We do not recommend that any teacher try to intervene physically without the help of other trained adults.

In some instances the teacher may feel the need to clear the room of everyone except the aggressive student and him- or herself. Two scenarios come to mind: The aggressive student is playing off his or her audience, and the safety of the other students is endangered. After the teacher sends the other students to another classroom, his or her involvement with the aggressive student should be calm and focused on preventing the behavior from escalating. Realistic limits need to be stated; for example, the teacher should inform the student that the police will be called in the event of assault. By talking to the student calmly and without an audience, the teacher who has developed rapport with the student may be able to calm the student down.

If a student becomes enraged at a teacher, the teacher should leave the area while the crisis response team intervenes. We have witnessed incidents in which team members have been injured when the person who was the target of the anger stayed with the team as they escorted the student to time-out.

Following any aggressive incident, the teacher should talk therapeutically with the student. Such communication can assist the student in dealing with his or her problems. The student may cry, go through a period of verbal venting, or simply calm down. In addition to talking with the student about the incident, the teacher should listen and assist the student in planning alternative behaviors for the next time a similar situation occurs. This step should never be overlooked, for at this time the student is most vulnerable to the idea of changing his or her behavior.

Knowing the symptoms of the different stages of frustration can help teachers recognize and circumvent aggressive behavior. But sometimes aggression will occur. The chapters that follow describe in detail specific strategies for dealing with verbal and physical aggression when it does occur.

▌ *DISCUSSION QUESTIONS*

1. As his students begin their written assignment, Mr. Gonzalez notices that John looks upset. He erases furiously and then stares at his paper with a blank look. How long should Mr. Gonzalez wait before he intervenes? What type of intervention should he try?
2. Bob has a short fuse. He is seated next to Sally, who for several days has been teasing him and then acting like what she did was no big deal. What can their teacher do to prevent Bob from blowing up at Sally?
3. Jimmy, a student in Mrs. Blum's class, hates history. He has not read the current assignment and does not know the answers to the quiz Mrs. Blum has just handed

out. His frustration increases, and without warning he picks up the quiz and throws it at his teacher. He then begins yelling that Mrs. Blum is the worst teacher he has ever had and that it is her fault that he could not pass the quiz. What should Mrs. Blum say or do in this situation?
4. As Mr. Santos walks down the hall he sees two high school boys fighting. What should he do?

▮ REFERENCES

Beck, M., Coleman, T., & Wineman, D. (1985). *Managing the unmanageable student.* Lexington, MA: Ginn Press.

Johns, B., Carr, V., & Hoots, C. (in press). *Reduction of school violence: Alternatives to suspension.* Horsham, PA: LRP Publications.

Schrumpf, F. (1991). *Peer mediation.* Champaign, IL: Research Press.

SIXTEEN TIPS FOR DEALING WITH AGGRESSIVE BEHAVIOR 6

■ 1. AN OUNCE OF PREVENTION IS WORTH A POUND OF CURE

The foremost technique educators can use in dealing with aggressive behavior is prevention, for, as the saying goes, an ounce of prevention is worth a pound of cure. When teachers and school administrators establish clear expectations and adopt high standards for behavior, they can prevent many behavior problems. All schools and classrooms should have clearly defined and stated rules or expectations.

Rules for students should be posted, explained, and reviewed with students on a periodic basis. In *The Garrison Model Handbook* (Garrison School Staff, 1994), school rules and expectations (cited in the Appendix) are reviewed at a whole-school assembly held at the beginning of the school year.

When school and classroom rules do not exist, discipline problems often abound. I am reminded of the time I led an in-service on dealing with behavioral problems at a school district that had many such problems. In the middle of the workshop, one of the teachers asked me what could be done about all the students who were running up and down the halls when they were supposed to be in class. I asked the teacher what the school rules were for appropriate hall behavior and was told there were no schoolwide rules. Consequently, I worked extensively with the district to establish clear whole-school and classroom expectations.

The more universal the rules are among the teachers of a school, the easier it is for students to behave appropriately. Being allowed to engage in a specific behavior in one class but not in another can only be confusing. One way to avoid this problem is for schools to develop a list of major infractions that have universal enforcement from all staff. The major infraction list is thoroughly explained to students at the beginning of the school year. A sample major infraction list is included in the Appendix.

Another preventive strategy is to look for signs of frustration or stress in students and intervene before situations become explosive. For instance, when students start to tap their pencils on the desk, to talk faster, or to rock back and forth in their chairs, it is wise to intervene. What can the teacher do? Sometimes it is enough for the teacher to let the students know that he or she is there to support them. A simple question such as "Can I help you with that?" may prevent a problem.

Proximity control is another effective prevention tool. By simply standing near a student who is frustrated or starting to argue with someone, a teacher can often diffuse the situation.

When a student who is unable to deal with his or her

frustration becomes defensive, the teacher can intervene by setting clear limits for the student or by asking the student to leave the situation. If a student behaving defensively becomes hostile in a given environment, the teacher can ask the student to run an errand or do something else to get the student out of the environment (Johns, Carr, & Hoots, in press).

■ *2. TEACHER TENSION CAN OFTEN AGITATE CRISIS BEHAVIOR*

When a student or classroom becomes agitated, it is not unusual for the teacher to feel tense and worry that he or she will not be able to deal with the situation. Showing tension is the worst thing a teacher can do, however; when the teacher becomes tense, so do the students, and thus they become even more agitated.

■ *3. ALWAYS REMAIN CALM*

It is vital that teachers remain cool, calm, and collected in crisis situations. Although remaining calm may be very difficult, it is critical that all of the students know the teacher is not getting upset over the situation.

■ *4. LOWER YOUR VOICE*

When dealing with any behavioral problem, the teacher should refrain from using a loud voice. Becoming loud will only escalate the problem. If a student becomes loud, the teacher should remain calm and deliberately lower his or her voice. Doing so will usually help calm the student. Often, however, when a student gets loud, the teacher gets louder to gain attention, then the student gets even louder, and before long a shouting match occurs. Nothing positive is accomplished; the situation simply gets worse.

▍ *5. SLOW YOUR RATE OF SPEECH*

When talking with a student who is upset, the teacher should slow his or her rate of speech. Often the tendency is to talk faster, but doing so will usually make the student more upset. In addition, when a student is upset, it may take him or her longer than usual to process what the teacher is saying. Slowing the rate of speech will help the situation.

▍ *6. ARRANGE THE ENVIRONMENT TO MINIMIZE RISKS*

If students in a class are prone to physical violence, the teacher should arrange the classroom environment in a way that will minimize risks. A student with a history of breaking windows should not be seated by a window. A student who is prone to darting out of doors should not be seated by the door.

Teachers must also think about what objects are accessible to students in the classroom. Knives used in a kitchen should not be within students' reach. Students in shop should be closely supervised when using power tools. Administrators and teachers should not leave money or keys around as a temptation to students.

We have found that students today require much closer supervision than ever before. Yet all too often when incidents occur in schools no adults are nearby.

7. STAND 1 ½ TO 3 FEET FROM A STUDENT WHO IS ACTING OUT—GIVE THE STUDENT SPACE

All people like others to respect their space, especially when they are angry. Students are no exception. In addition to not violating a student's space, the teacher should refrain from touching a student who is angry. Teachers are more likely to get hit if they touch an angry student.

8. BE AWARE OF YOUR BODY STANCE

A teacher should not stand face-to-face, eyeball-to-eyeball, with a student who is angry. His or her stance will be taken as confrontational, as asking for a fight. It is better to stand at an angle and to the side of the student.

9. DRESS IN A MANNER THAT MINIMIZES RISK OF INJURY

Female teachers should avoid wearing dangling earrings. Students can too easily pull on an earring if they are upset, slitting the ear permanently. Male teachers may want to avoid neckties. If a student gets angry, he or she can grab the necktie and choke the teacher.

10. REMIND MISBEHAVING STUDENTS OF THE CONSEQUENCE OF THEIR BEHAVIOR

A misbehaving student should always receive a warning about the consequence of continuing the inappropriate behavior.

11. ALLOW VERBAL VENTING

Quite some time ago a student came to our high school

as a junior. She was used to getting her way by calling people names and ranting and raving. When she first came to our school, she would often yell and scream for two hours straight. We found that she needed to be removed from the classroom after five minutes of starting this behavior. She would be escorted to the time-out room and told that we would talk to her after she had calmed down. We would then turn away from her (careful that we could still see what she was doing). At first she would yell for two hours. Only after she was quiet for five minutes would we talk to her about appropriate behavior in the classroom. Soon she learned that yelling and screaming were not going to get her attention. We suggest that teachers allow verbal venting but remove the agitated student from any audience so that he or she cannot disrupt the rest of the class or school.

■ *12. IGNORE IRRELEVANT COMMENTS; REDIRECT THE STUDENT BACK TO THE PROBLEM AT HAND*

Some students will do everything possible to manipulate the teacher and get him or her "off track." They will make such comments as, "You didn't make Jimmy finish his math work" and "When Sally did that, you didn't do anything to her." The teacher must be careful to not get drawn into those arguments. Instead, the teacher should calmly repeat exactly what he or she wants the student to do using behavior specific dialogue, as outlined in this book.

■ *13. PROVIDE CHOICES*

Students are quick to blame others and often will not accept that anything is their fault. One way a teacher can place the responsibility for their actions on their shoulders is to give them choices and show them that they are the ones making the choices. For instance, if a student is out of control in the classroom, the teacher can say, "You may go to the time-out room on your own, or I will get assistance to take you there—it's your choice." If the student goes on his or her own, the teacher should thank the student for making a good choice.

▌ *14. SET LIMITS*

As we will discuss in Chapter 7, an important component of dialogue is setting time limits for students. By setting time limits, the teacher provides structure for students who desperately need it. Words like "I will give you five seconds to decide" work well with many students.

▌ *15. USE PHYSICAL RESTRAINT TECHNIQUES AS A LAST RESORT*

We believe in using safe physical restraint as a last resort when students are endangering themselves or others. If safe physical restraint is to be used in a school district, a team of individuals in each school should be trained in its use. In addition, the district must establish written policies concerning the use of safe physical restraint. For special education students, restraint procedures should be included in the behavioral management plan.

▌ *16. ONCE THE STUDENT IS CALM, USE THE INCIDENT TO TEACH ALTERNATIVE, APPROPRIATE WAYS TO DEAL WITH AGGRESSION*

In the school setting, teachers must use each incident

of aggression as a teaching opportunity. After an incident has occurred, the teacher must talk with the student about what happened, how the student handled the situation, and what he or she could do differently the next time a similar situation occurs. The teacher and student should discuss options other than the use of aggression. Teachers cannot assume that students know other ways of dealing with anger; it is often necessary to teach such techniques.

■ *THE GARRISON MODEL*

Throughout the book, we frequently refer to the Garrison Model. The Garrison Model is a therapeutic program that continually emphasizes a student's responsibility for the choices that he or she makes. This approach to dealing with students with behavior disorders has proven effective in reducing violence and inappropriate behaviors of the students enrolled in the Garrison School, located in Jacksonville, Illinois.

The Model was developed at the Garrison School, a public, alternative day school that serves students identified as having severe behavior disorders. In addition to the emphasis on students' responsibility for their actions, other key components of the school include:

- I the whole-school approach
- I direct social skills training
- I positive involvement in the community through Community Service Learning
- I elimination of suspension coupled with the development of logical and natural consequences for inappropriate behavior
- I interagency coordination
- I safe school planning

- gang identification
- intervention and prevention
- creating a positive environment
- positive acknowledgment of student success
- violence intervention through the team approach
- developing good community public relations
- accenting the positive

▮ *DISCUSSION QUESTIONS*

1. How many of the tips discussed in this chapter do you use regularly in dealing with aggressive students?
2. Think about the last time you had to deal with an incident of aggression in your classroom. How did you handle it? What might have you done differently?

▮ *REFERENCES*

Garrison School Staff. (1994). *The Garrison Model Handbook*. Garrison School, 936 W. Michigan, Jacksonville, IL 62650.

Johns, B., Carr, V., & Hoots, C. (in press). *Reduction of school violence: Alternatives to suspension*. Horsham, PA: LRP Publications.

DEALING WITH VERBAL AGGRESSION 7

*T*he teacher is the model for all students. How the teacher talks to students sets an example for the entire school; it can prevent an inappropriate behavior or cause it to escalate.

Many ways of talking to students are not effective. For example, if a student is running in the hall and the teacher says "Wouldn't you like to quit running?" the student will most likely not stop running. Likewise, if the teacher begs a student to do something by saying "Come on, please," or something along those lines, the student is not likely to do what the teacher wants. The "Mr. or Mrs. Nice Guy" approach is ineffective.

So is the "tough guy" approach. Statements like "You had better get that work done" or "Now you have had it" will typically result in the student testing the teacher to see what he or she will do.

Another ineffective way of talking to students is to use words like "Okay, okay—it's all right this time but don't let it happen again." The student will see the teacher as a weak individual and will lose respect.

When teachers tell students to do something over and over again, the students will often ignore them. Requesting something over and over again seldom produces the intended results.

As mentioned previously, we advocate the use of behavior specific dialogue. In our experience it has worked consistently, even with students with severe behavioral problems. This procedure was adapted from Jenson, Reavis, and Rhode (1992) by Johns, Carr, and Hoots (in press).

The procedure (Figure 7.1) calls for making no more than two "I" request statements. For example, suppose a teacher wants a student to stay in his or her seat in class. The teacher tells the student, "I need you to sit in your seat," and then waits for five seconds. When dealing with elementary-age students, it is recommended that the teacher count to five out loud. For students who are in junior or senior high school, the teacher should look at his or her watch for five seconds. If the student complies with the teacher's request, the teacher should say, "Thank you—I appreciate that you are in your seat." If the student does not comply, the teacher should state one more time, "I need you to sit in your seat, and should then wait another five seconds. If the student complies, the teacher should say, "Thank you—I appreciate it." If the student does not comply, the teacher should administer the applicable consequence.

When dealing with any behavioral problem, the teacher should, as mentioned previously, refrain from using a loud voice and slow his or her rate of speech. The teacher should not argue with a student who is upset; he or she is not going to listen. Rather, the teacher should state in a calm voice, "I will talk to you when you are calm," and then let the

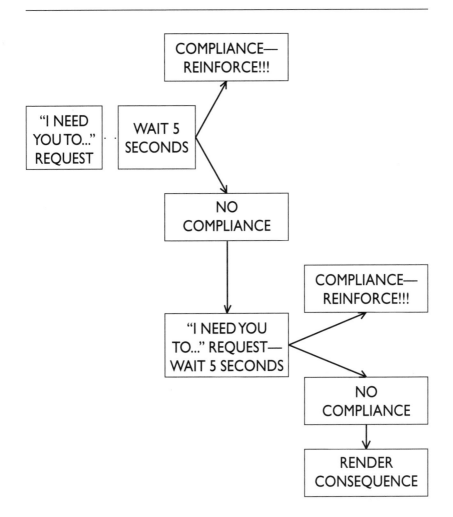

Adapted from Jenson, Reavis, and Rhode (1992) by Johns, Carr, and Hoots (in press).

FIGURE 7.1
Behavior Specific Dialogue

student verbally vent.

Should a student be allowed to vent in front of other students? In most instances, no. The student should not have an audience. The teacher should do everything possible to remove the student from the situation and get the student someplace alone where he or she can verbally vent and calm down. If the student refuses to move or to leave the situation, the teacher should provide the student with a choice: "You may either leave the room on your own with me or I will get assistance to escort you from the room." The student should be given five seconds to decide. If the student moves on his or her own, the teacher should say, "Thank you for making a good choice." If the student does not move, the teacher will have to seek assistance to remove the student from the room. The use of physical guidance should be used only as a last resort, when all other methods have been unsuccessful. Physical guidance and restraint techniques are discussed later in this book.

As we have noted before, it is important that teachers set clear limits for students. Giving students a choice and setting a limit of five seconds to comply provides the structure that many of today's students need and want (Johns et al., in press).

▮ *DISCUSSION QUESTIONS*

1. Think about the last time you dealt with a student who was verbally aggressive. Did you use "I" statements?
2. In the same instance, how many times did you ask the student to do whatever it was that you wanted him or her to do? Did you remain calm and lower your voice?

∎ *REFERENCES*

Jenson, W., Reavis, K., & Rhode, G. (1992). *Magic in a classroom: Practical research valid interventions.* (Workshop handout.) Salt Lake City: University of Utah.

Johns, B., Carr, V., & Hoots, C. (in press). *Reduction of school violence: Alternatives to suspension.* Horsham, PA: LRP Publications.

USE OF TIME-OUT 8

Time-out is a widely misused and misunderstood be-havior management technique. However, if fully understood, it can be used effectively in the school. We advocate its use as outlined in this chapter.

Operationally defined, "time-out" refers to the con-tingent withdrawal of those reinforcing stimuli thought to be maintaining the behavior of concern (Garrison School Staff, 1994). When time-out is used correctly, all chances of positive reinforcement for the student are removed in an effort to decrease the undesired behavior.

Unfortunately, many teachers use time-out incorrectly. Often, they will send the misbehaving student out to the hall. But that does not remove all chances of positive re-inforcement. In most schools a student sitting in the hall will receive a lot of attention; the student may actually prefer to sit in the hall than be in the classroom. Another com-mon place for time-out is the principal's office. But there, too, all chances of positive reinforcement are not removed. The secretary is on the phone, students are coming in and out, the principal is talking to visitors. Neither the hallway nor the principal's office is an appropriate place for time-out. Use of those areas for this purpose may cause inappropriate behavior to escalate in the classroom; students may begin to misbehave out of a *desire* to receive time-out.

It is important to remember that time-out is effective only if the teacher follows it with reinforcing the student for the opposite, appropriate behavior. Take, for instance, Mrs. Brown. She is having a lot of difficulty with Johnny, who is very loud (screaming) in the classroom. She decides to use time-out. But time-out alone is not sufficient. She must also recognize and praise Johnny when he is being quiet in the classroom.

An integral part of the time-out procedure is deciding how long to allow a disruptive behavior to continue before intervening. Five to ten minutes is often appropriate, but we have worked with teachers who have allowed students to disrupt the classroom for a solid hour before intervening. An hour is much too long a time to allow a student to disrupt a classroom.

Before a school adopts a time-out procedure or a teacher uses time-out for a child in the classroom, the school administrator or teacher must notify the parent(s) that this procedure will be used. Before it is used with a special education student, time-out must be specified in the student's individualized education program (IEP) as part of the behavioral management plan. All schools should have a policy or procedural statement concerning the use of time-out. An example is provided in the Appendix.

In 1992 a school district in Illinois was sued because a teacher placed a student in a locked three-foot by three-foot box. This time-out setting was completely inappropriate. The incident highlights the necessity of using ethical and legal procedures.

Students must be informed about the specific behaviors that will lead to time-out before the procedure is ever used. They must also be told the consequences for engaging in those behaviors and must be given a warning before the consequence is implemented. And following any time-out procedure the student must be given the chance to clarify the behavior that led to time-out and to identify and practice alternative behaviors.

Time-out does not need to involve removing the child from the classroom. Different levels of isolation can be used. We suggest using the following four levels.

The first level is ignoring the child who is behaving inappropriately but allowing him or her to remain in the classroom. An example is not attending to a student who is calling out without raising his or her hand. However, the teacher must also reinforce the student when he or she acts appropriately.

The second level is used commonly with primary-age students. The teacher has the misbehaving student place his or her head on the desk for a short, specified period of time.

The third level of isolation is to separate the student engaging in inappropriate behavior from the setting in which the behavior occurs but having the student remain in the classroom. The student may be told to sit in a corner, in an isolated study carrel, or behind a partition.

The second and third levels are means of in-class self-removal. The desk or other designated area of the room serves as a "quiet corner," or area in which the student can regain composure.

The key for success of an in-room time-out is the removal of reinforcement to the student. However, many students gain reinforcement by the sounds and actions around them even when they cannot participate. Some cannot resist talking to others. For these students, in-room time-out is not very successful.

The fourth, most restrictive level is to send the student to a time-out room. We developed the following standards for time-out rooms:

1. They should be constructed of materials acceptable as fire-safe by the school district.
2. The floor should be at least four feet by four feet and the ceiling at least seven feet high.
3. They should be properly lighted and ventilated.
4. They should be free of objects and fixtures with which children can harm themselves.
5. There should be a means by which an adult can continuously monitor, visually and auditorily, the student's behavior. Students should be supervised at all times while in the time-out room.
6. They should be unlocked or have no door.

Level four time-out should be implemented only when a student is disrupting the class to the point that the teacher cannot teach and the rest of the class cannot learn. The teacher should stress to all students that the classroom is a place for students to learn and that those who disrupt the learning process to the extent that others cannot learn must leave the classroom until they regain their ability to act in an appropriate manner. The time-out room should not be used as a penalty box but rather as a quiet area in which a student can regain self-control.

The following example illustrates appropriate dialogue for imposing a level four time-out. Note the behavior specific language. Justin has begun using an inappropriate tone of voice, is refusing to work, and has started calling the teacher names. The teacher provides a warning to Justin: "I need you to get quiet and complete your work or you will need to go to time-out." If Justin were to quiet down, the teacher would say: "Thank you, I appreciate your getting back to work." But Justin continues to call the teacher names. The teacher says one more time: "I need you to get quiet and complete your work or you will need to go to time-out." Again, if Justin were to get back to work and become quiet, the teacher would reinforce his behavior. But Justin simply yells louder, shouting: "I'm not going to time-out, and you can't make me." In truth, he is right, for Justin weighs 250 pounds. The teacher knows he needs to give Justin a choice. He says, "You may either walk to the time-out room on your own or I will get assistance to take you there." The teacher then counts to five. Justin decides to walk on his own, and the teacher thanks him for making a good choice. If Justin had refused to move, the teacher would have called the crisis response team to escort Justin to the time-out room. The use of a team and physical intervention is discussed in detail later in this book.

All teachers who use time-out as a behavior management strategy should post the time-out room rules. Those suggested in the Garrison Model (Garrison School Staff, 1994) are as follows:

1. Students will refrain from talking or yelling to anyone outside the time-out room.
2. Students will refrain from touching the light switches, smoke alarm, and dividers.
3. Students will stand away from the doorway or wherever the staff member indicates.
4. Students will sit or stand to take their time. Students will not sleep.

5. Students will not take any objects (pencils, pens, purses, coats, etc.) into the time-out room. If objects such as keys or coins, etc., are thrown, they will be held until the end of the day.
6. Students who are out of control will not have personal items that may cause injury (belts, shoes, earrings, etc.) in time-out.
7. Students may not do homework in the time-out room.
8. Students should have five minutes of calm, appropriate behavior before returning to class. (Students who refuse to return will have the option of returning on their own or being escorted.)

If a student in the time-out room continues to yell, the staff should not engage the student in conversation. More effective is to let the student know that he or she must calm down and remain calm for a specified period of time (we recommend five minutes) before anyone will speak with him or her. The staff should calmly tell the student: "When you are quiet, you need to ask me to start your time." If the student becomes quiet and asks, in an appropriate tone of voice, for his or her time to be started, the five minutes should begin. If, however, the student starts yelling again, the staff should repeat the process. It is important to limit the time that a student spends in time-out, however. Some students will use time-out to avoid class work or to get out of a class. If a teacher suspects a student is using time-out in this way, one option is to hold the student at his or her desk. This technique is discussed in Chapter 10. Another option for the teacher is to issue a warning that the student will have to make up, after school, the instructional time missed from class if he or she is sent to time-out more than two times during the day. This consequence places the responsibility for the behavior back on the student and helps to ensure that time-out is used appropriately.

The teacher must be consistent in enforcing the expectation that the student stand or sit quietly and appropriately in the time-out room. Further, the teacher should never argue with a student in (or out of) time-out. The teacher is the professional; the teacher knows that he or she is right and does not need to prove it to the student. The teacher gave the student the chance to make a good decision.

Many students will try to get the teacher to argue with them. They are trying to make the teacher angry and frustrated. When a student begins to manipulate a teacher in this way, the teacher should remove him- or herself from the argument and say, "I will talk to you when you are calm."

After a student has served his or her five minutes of quiet time, the teacher should engage in problem solving with the student. It is important to discuss the incident that resulted in the student going to the time-out room and the behavior that is expected in the classroom. Students tend to respond best to life-space interviews* immediately after they become calm. Teachers should take advantage of this time to discuss more appropriate choices the student can make in the future. Often, when alternative choices and their consequences are discussed, the "real" problem surfaces.

Because people most clearly remember the last thing they hear, we recommend ending the discussion with posi-

---

* A life-space interview is a therapeutic, verbal strategy for use with students in crisis. The talk helps students see the connections between their feelings and their behavior (Wood & Young, 1991).

tive statements. Rather than saying, "I do not want to see you hit Johnny again," the teacher should end the conversation with, "I know you can ignore Johnny's pestering if this situation begins again." The teacher should give students the feeling that they can do the right thing in the classroom or school and that the teacher believes in them.

After the incident has been discussed, it is over. Although it is easy to hold grudges, doing so does nothing to improve the situation. When the student walks into school the next day, the worst thing the teacher can say is: "I hope today is better than yesterday." It is much better to say: "Good morning! Let's all work to have a good day today."

Remember that no matter what students have done in the past, when they are behaving, they deserve the teacher's help, respect, smiles, and acceptance. Teachers should avoid sending signals that their students' appropriate behavior is not appreciated.

Finally, any situation that has required the use of time-out should be documented. A sample form can found in the Appendix. Documentation should include time, date, student name, file number, and a brief description of the incident. The names of staff members involved in the incident should also be noted. A copy of the report should be placed in the student's file.

▮ *DISCUSSION QUESTIONS*

1. Have you used any form of time-out with your students? If so, which level of time-out have you used?
2. In your opinion, was your use of time-out effective? Why or why not?
3. Have you used level four time-out? If so, where was the time-out area?

∎ *REFERENCES*

Garrison School Staff. (1994). *The Garrison Model Handbook.* Garrison School, 936 W. Michigan, Jacksonville, IL 62650.

Wood, M., & Young, N. (1991). *Life space intervention.* Austin, TX: PRO-ED.

BULLY-PROOFING YOUR CLASSROOM 9

*T*his week, I observed several instances of bullying in a kindergarten class. Among them: One student stood over another, smaller youngster and demanded that he give him the toy he was playing with or he would "get him." Another child, who wanted to be in the front of the line of students, gave another child a mean look and pushed him out of the way.

In this morning's newspaper, an article told the story of two 11-year-old children who tried to bully a 5-year-old into stealing candy from a store for them. They became angry when the child refused to comply. They lured the 5-year-old and his 8-year-old brother into a vacant four-teenth-floor apartment and again demanded that they steal for them. When the brothers refused, they dangled the younger brother out the window. The older brother attempted to save him, but after a struggle, the 5-year-old fell and died from massive head injuries. Admittedly, this case of bullying is extreme, but it leads one to wonder how young those 11-year-olds were when they started this pattern of behavior.

DeBruyn and Larson (1984) described the school bully as the student who pushes people around, both verbally and physically; who threatens others; who brags loudly about his or her strength; who is extremely negative; who talks back, usually very publicly announcing what he or she plans to do; who degrades and humiliates others in public view; and who looks for trouble.

Other insights into schoolyard bullying and victimization were provided by authorities in these areas who attended the Schoolyard Bully Practicum, which was sponsored by the National School Safety Center and held at Harvard in May 1987. Their conclusions, reported in the School Safety Check Book (National School Safety Center, 1990b), included the following:

- School bullying is a significant and pervasive problem.
- Fear and suffering are becoming a way of life for victims of bullying.
- Young bullies are more likely to become criminals as adults and to suffer from family and professional problems.
- The prevailing attitude that kids fighting each other are just experiencing normal youthful aggressive behavior must be discarded.
- The United States should follow the lead of Scandinavia and Japan, whose governments have addressed bullying problems with national intervention and prevention programs. (p. 125)

Similarly, Leonard Eron, a psychologist at the University of Illinois at Chicago who studied bullying behavior in a group of subjects over a twenty-two-year period, found that young bullies had approximately a 1 in 4 chance of having a criminal record by age 30 whereas nonbullying children had about a 1 in 20 chance of having an adult criminal record (National School Safety Center, 1990b).

The results of a survey conducted in the spring and summer of 1990 of 204 middle and high school students from several small, rural, seemingly safe midwestern communities clearly show the magnitude of the problem. Hazler, Hoover, and Oliver (1993) reported that 75% of the students surveyed said they had been bullied and 90% of those bullied said they had suffered side effects such as a drop in grades and an increase in anxiety. Middle school students reported the highest levels of bullying.

Despite these findings, teachers and administrators have tended to ignore this problem. From our experience, we believe that no form of aggression should be ignored. Low-level aggression allowed to continue becomes high-level aggression.

Bullying affects both the classroom and school climate. Students who have been the victims of bullying become afraid to go to school or, as reported by the National School Safety Center (1990a), are far more likely than other students to bring a weapon to school to protect themselves.

What steps can educators take to stop bullying? We recommend the following.

1. Through surveys and conversations with students, staff, and parents, educators should assess the problem in the classroom or school. How many children believe they are victims of bullying? What names are discussed when bullying is mentioned? How do students perceive the school's response to bullying—do they believe teachers know about it and do nothing or do not care? Has the school done anything when problems have been brought up?

   Educators need to listen when parents report instances of bullying. A school in our area set a poor example. When a parent, upset by the bullying behavior of a student toward her child, reported the incident to the school, the principal informed her that "it was nothing."

2. Educators should establish clear rules or expectations that bullying is not acceptable in the school setting. They need to send the message to children that hurting other students physically or psychologically will not be tolerated. They must also establish set consequences for different types of bullying.

3. Educators should not ignore any bullying incident; by ignoring bullying, educators are condoning it.

4. If a student is caught bullying, another student or group of students, he or she should be sent to an appropriate time-out area for a short period of time. After the student has served the time-out, the teacher needs to talk with the student about the consequences established for bullying, about the choice the student made, and about more appropriate behaviors. It is much better to confront the bully in private than in front of the classroom. Bullies want to be in control and gain power; calling attention to the behavior in front of peers may give the bullying student more power.

5. The predetermined consequence should be imposed. Consequences for bullying may include the loss of a privilege, such as having to wait until last to line up and not being able to go in the restroom at the same time as the other students. If the bullying occurred during recess, the student may lose so many minutes of recess time. If the bullying occurred on the bus, the student may be assigned a seat close to the driver.

6. The parents of the student who is bullying and the parents of the student who is the victim should be notified. The parents of the bully should be encouraged

to work with the school to monitor their child's activities and should be encouraged to provide positive reinforcement when the child is acting appropriately. The parents of the victim of bullying should be encouraged to work with the school to teach their child appropriate ways of handling the situation, including how to act assertively.

7. To reduce the opportunities for bullying, educators should closely monitor the classroom, playground, cafeteria, and restrooms. Because we have found that bullying increases when students are lining up for activities, are walking to and from the bus, are on the bus, and are walking to and from school, these settings should also be supervised as much as possible.

   Some schools have hired additional hall monitors. Some have placed video equipment in the hallways and on the buses. Some have elicited the support of local police departments in watching for signs of problems before and after school.

8. Because of the bully's need for attention and power, it is important for educators to reinforce the bully when he or she is acting appropriately. Good behavior should never be taken for granted. To increase the positive behavior of the child who was bullying but is now behaving appropriately, educators must reinforce that student and recognize the student for what he or she is doing right.

9. Educators must also teach appropriate social skills. Programs such as Goldstein's *Aggression Replacement Training* (Goldstein & Glick, 1987) and *Skillstreaming* (Goldstein, Sprafkin, Gershaw, & Klein, 1980; McGinnis & Goldstein, 1984) are excellent resources. Problem-solving techniques should be taught to bul-

lies, victims, and onlookers. Cooperative behavior and conflict resolution (Chapter 5) should be encouraged and reinforced.

10. Most important, educators must be models for the behavior they want their students to exhibit. They cannot use intimidation tactics to manage student behavior. Educators who use nonconfrontational techniques yet are firm, fair, and consistent are modeling appropriate behavior for students.

▌ DISCUSSION QUESTIONS

1. Think about the students in your classroom. Are any of them bullies? If so, describe their behavior.
2. When and where does bullying occur among your students? Have you been ignoring it? What have you been doing to stop it?
3. What are the consequences in your classroom for bullying?
4. When bullying has occurred in your classroom or among your students, have you notified the parents of the bully and the victim?

▌ REFERENCES

DeBruyn, R., & Larson, J. (1984). *You can handle them all.* Manhattan, KS: The Master Teacher.

Goldstein, A., & Glick, B. (1987). *Aggression replacement training: A comprehensive intervention for aggressive youth.* Champaign, IL: Research Press.

Goldstein, A., Sprafkin, R., Gershaw, N., & Klein, P. (1980). *Skillstreaming the adolescent.* Champaign, IL: Research Press.

Hazler, R., Hoover, J., & Oliver, R. (1993). What do kids say about bullying? *Education Digest, 58*(7), 16-20.

McGinnis, E., & Goldstein, A. (1984). *Skillstreaming the elementary school child*. Champaign, IL: Research Press.

National School Safety Center. (1990a). *Safe schools overview*. Malibu, CA: National School Safety Center, Pepperdine University.

National School Safety Center. (1990b). *School safety check book*. Malibu, CA: National School Safety Center, Pepperdine University.

DEALING WITH PHYSICAL AGGRESSION 10

*A*ll students need to know that the learning environment is a safe place. They must feel that the administration and staff have established a workable plan for preventing violence and for dealing with aggressive students. Being prepared to professionally deal with student aggression is in itself a deterrent against aggression. But when aggression does occur, physical intervention may be necessary. This chapter provides general tips for safe physical intervention.

▮ GUIDELINES FOR ADMINISTRATORS AND STAFF

Every school should establish a policy regarding the use of physical intervention with students who are out of control and require physical escorting or holding. It should outline the actual processes of physical intervention, and staff should be trained in those processes. All staff should follow the policy guidelines whenever physical intervention is warranted.

Most policies consider physical intervention appropriate when students are endangering themselves or others or are so out of control that they are damaging property or interfering with the educational process. Policies generally designate the number of staff members suggested for safe intervention; the specific staff members who should be involved; verbal intervention options to consider before the use of physical intervention; procedures for safety; and procedures for documentation. A sample policy specifically geared toward safe physical restraint is included in the Appendix.

In any instance of physical aggression, if endangerment is not an issue, we recommend trying verbal interventions first. Using behavior specific dialogue the teacher can give the student the opportunity to leave the area or stop his or her aggressive behavior. It is important to remember that when adults employ physical intervention they are taking over the student's ability to control him- or herself. Physical intervention should be used only as a last resort.

Students who are losing control need clear, concise directions regarding their behavior. Such directions can be provided with behavior specific dialogue. The teacher should specify a short but appropriate amount of time for student compliance and should keep the student informed of how much time has elapsed. Once the process has begun, it is important to follow through. Students are always given the option of controlling their own behavior. However, if they are unable to do so, physical intervention will be necessary to keep them from hurting themselves or others.

We recommend using a team approach to physical intervention and suggest including as many people on the team as necessary to ensure everyone's safety. We have found that teams of four to five adults work well. One adult can hold each arm and leg and the fifth adult can support the student's head and shoulders. Using five adults thus ensures the safety of both the student and the staff. With small or young students, fewer adults may be needed. With large students, six to eight staff members may be required. At all times safety should be the primary concern. Guidelines for setting up an intervention team are included in Chapter 14 (Johns & Carr, 1994).

We also recommend that staff wear latex gloves during physical intervention to minimize the risk of blood contamination. Staff members in schools with high levels of aggressive behavior should carry gloves in their pockets at all times. Some schools have reported that students who were acting aggressively became compliant when staff put on gloves in preparation for intervention (Garrison School Staff, 1994). Many students do not want to be touched by adults wearing latex gloves.

Another safety precaution is to have soft leather helmets close at hand to put on students who head-bang to inflict self-injury. We have found that helmets similar to those used by students with developmental delays for the prevention of injury work well with students in crisis. Even after securing the helmet on a student, the staff may need to hold the student's head to prevent injury.

Several other pieces of advice are crucial. Educators should never warn of the use of physical intervention unless the situation warrants it, they are willing to follow through, and they are capable of doing so. At times when buildings are short of staff it may be humanly impossible to safely intervene. At such times physical intervention should not be offered as a consequence.

When using physical intervention, educators should act professionally and seriously. Physical intervention is an action that should not be taken lightly. It is also important that professional staff work as a team to ensure safety. Highly aggressive students, in particular, may try to bait one staff member into intervening alone. The student may say something like, "You think you're so big and bad. Why don't you make me go to time-out!" Staff must be on guard against this type of baiting. The response from the staff should be a calm statement such as, "In this school we work as team. No one person will force another person to do anything."

In addition to ensuring safety, the team approach makes it difficult for the student to blame any one individual for the intervention. The Garrison School staff (1994) reported that their students, who have severe behavioral disorders have maintained respect for and have developed a sense of rapport with the crisis response team members. They attribute this attitude to the professional manner in which the team intervenes with the students.

Finally, the team approach means that there will be adult witnesses in the event that a student later claims a staff member intentionally inflicted injury.

SELF-DEFENSE TECHNIQUES

When a student is upset, he or she may bite, kick, pull hair, punch, or act aggressively in other ways. This section describes self-defense techniques staff members can use to avoid personal injury from these acts of aggression.

Bites

Young children especially, but even junior and senior high school students, have been known to bite teachers and staff. To release a bite, the teacher can push the hand that is being bitten further into the student's mouth as he or she is biting. The inward push to the mouth causes the jaw to open and the bite to release. The teacher should immediately wash any cut, scratched, or torn skin with antibacterial soap.

Hair Pulls

Younger students also tend to pull hair. The best response to prevent hair loss is for the staff member whose hair is being pulled to push his or her head toward the student doing the hair pulling. This movement will unbalance the student and cause him or her to release the grip. As the staff member moves toward the student, he or she can place a hand over the student's hand, pressing it against his or her head. The student will no longer be able to pull the staff member's hair. We recommend that the staff member get assistance for releasing the student's hand once it has been secured against the staff member's head.

Wrist Grabs

The weakest point in a grab is between the thumb and index finger. If a student grabs a staff member's wrist, the staff member should twist his or her wrist in the direction of the hold where the student's thumb and index finger meet. Simultaneously, he or she should move away from the grab. Staff can try this technique on themselves by grabbing their own wrist and twisting out and away from the grab.

Two-Handed Wrist Grabs

If a student grabs a staff member's arm with two hands, the staff member should make a fist with the arm that is grabbed, place his or her other hand over the fist, and pull upward and to the side out of the grab. This technique takes practice. We recommend that staff practice with a partner.

Chokes

If a student tries to choke a staff member from the front, the staff member should very quickly raise both of his or her arms outside the student's arms and twist away from the hold. As the staff member twists away, his or her arms will knock the student's hands away from the throat. The staff member can also yell to startle the student. He or she should not, however, try to struggle to release the student's hands.

If a student tries to choke a staff member from the back, he or she should again rapidly raise both arms outside the student's arms, but this time the staff member should twist toward the student to break the hold.

In any choking incident in which a student is attacking a teacher, as soon as the teacher is free he or she should leave the area and seek adult help. Often the student will have targeted that teacher; the attack most likely was not random.

Kicks

If a student begins to kick a staff member in the leg, the staff member should quickly turn to the side, raise his or her leg, and bend it at the knee. These actions will allow the staff member's leg to "give with the blow" should it be kicked. Keeping one's leg rigidly planted on the floor will increase the likelihood of a broken bone. As with choking, the staff member should immediately get away from the situation and seek assistance.

Punches

If a student throws a punch at a staff member, the staff

member should try to grab the student's fist as the punch is thrown and pull it past his or her body. The staff member will be using the momentum of the punch to pull the student past him or her. While pulling the punch through, the staff member should move in the opposite direction and get away. He or she should then seek adult help.

Although these descriptions of self-defense for the classroom are brief, they can be very helpful. We recommend that all educators take part in several practice sessions for each technique to feel comfortable in its use.

ESCORTING STUDENTS

Frequently, students in crisis need to be removed from a classroom (or other situation) to get themselves calm. Often, however, they will want to save face and will refuse to leave. The recommended method of escorting a student from an area is through team intervention. The teacher in charge should, using behavior specific dialogue, ask the student to leave. If, after the two requests, the student does not leave the area, the crisis response team should be summoned. The team leader will instruct the team about who should take what position and will then lead the team in physically guiding the student away from the area.

With the preferred method of escorting, one staff member holds the student's right arm, and another his or her left arm, straight away from the side of the student's body. They hold the student with one hand on the student's wrist and the other under the armpit. The student's palms should face the ceiling. The staff members then walk the student quickly through the hall with two other team members following behind to provide assistance should the student become violent. As they walk, the staff holding the student gently lift the student onto his or her tiptoes. This puts the student slightly off balance and provides safer transport. When the team reaches the destination, the student is released.

This intervention works well with both younger and older students. We recommend that the team transporting students always consists of four adults.

■ *PHYSICAL INTERVENTION*

Often what comes to mind when physical intervention is mentioned is full-blown physical restraint in which the student is restrained on the floor. However, there are several alternatives to floor restraint that often work equally well for calming a student when physical intervention is necessary. Among these are the desk hold, the corner hold, and the sitting hold. Floor restraint, in our opinion, should be used only as a last resort.

The Desk Hold

For agitated students who cannot remain quiet in the classroom and who do not use the time-out room appropriately, the Garrison Model (Garrison School Staff, 1994) recommends the desk hold, a form of in-class intervention. This type of intervention is appropriate for students who are out of control, perhaps throwing books or yelling, and who refuse to calm down even after behavior specific dialogue is used.

With this approach, two team members stand beside the student at his or her desk and hold the student's arms out to either side and flat against the desk. Two other team members stand behind the desk, place their feet behind the legs of the student's chair, and they hold the student's shoulders and chair. The team leader asks the student to let the team know when he or she is ready to start his or her time. As soon as the student asks appropriately that the time be started, the staff counts out one minute per arm and releases each arm as the time expires if the student has remained quiet. The team waits until the student begins engaging in appropriate class behavior and following through with the directive that was given prior to the team's involvement. Once the student has begun to comply, the team quietly exits the room. During the intervention there is little talking and the rest of the class members continue on with their school work.

To stop a student from yelling or swearing, a team member can gently push up under the student's chin to close the student's mouth. Typically this intervention is carried out only to prevent the student from disrupting the rest of the class. All of the crisis response team members should wear latex gloves.

The Garrison School staff (1994) reported a high level of success with the desk hold for older as well as younger students. They found that most students would avoid behavior that would result in intervention in front of their peers. This method also worked well with students who, after returning from the time-out room, resumed misbehaving and those who made a game out of use of the time-out room.

The intervention is also a safe method for holding pregnant students. Care must be taken that no pressure is put on any part of the stomach or abdomen.

With older students, four to six staff members may be needed to hold the student. Also, certain desks work better than others. The Garrison School staff found that they were best able to hold the student's arms on the desk when the desktop had a slight overhang. With such desks, they could hook their fingertips under the overhang and securely hold the student's arm while placing very little pressure on the arm (Johns & Carr, 1994).

The Corner Hold

Another option to a floor restraint for students who become violent and do not respond to verbal intervention is the corner hold. With this approach the crisis response team members walk the student to a corner of the room and cross the student's arms in front of his or her chest. Two staff members hold the student's crossed arms at the wrist and turn the student so he or she is facing the corner. Other staff members plant their feet behind the student's feet to prevent kicking. They may also place their shoulders against the student's sides so the student stands securely. When the student becomes calm the team leader asks the student to say when he or she is ready to start his or her time. As with the desk hold, as soon as the student asks appropriately, the staff times one minute for each arm, releasing the arm at the end of the minute.

If the student becomes violent and begins to kick or head-bang, a staff member should lift one of the student's legs upward from the knee. This position places the student off balance and will not allow the student to kick. In addition, the student's shoes should be removed. They can be returned when the student calms down (Johns & Carr, 1994).

The Sitting Hold

A third option to floor restraint is the sitting hold. This physical intervention works well with students who are overweight or prone to head-banging. When a student is too large to hold safely in a standing position in the corner, the crisis response team can sit the student in the middle of the floor with his or her legs extended straight out in front. Staff members kneeling behind the student hold the student's arms, crossed in front of the student, at the wrists. Other team members gently hold the student's shoulders slightly forward.

As with the other holds, the team leader asks the student to say when he or she is ready to start his or her time. After the student asks appropriately, the staff begin to time one minute per arm and release each arm as the time expires.

With each of these interventions, after the student is released, he or she should take five minutes to quietly stand or sit in the time-out room. Following the quiet time, a staff member should talk with the student and bring the situation to closure before the student returns to the classroom.

We recommend intense training for staff interested in using these techniques. At all times student and staff safety should be the primary concern. To recap our safety concerns, we recommend that any physical intervention come from a team of four to five trained individuals; latex gloves be worn for the protection of all involved; a helmet be used for students who head-bang; and training be given to the team in intervention methods. We also recommend that alternatives such as a desk, corner, and sitting restraints be employed whenever possible instead of floor restraint (Johns & Carr, 1994).

▮ STAFF ATTITUDE AND FEELINGS

The following guidelines may be helpful for maintaining a professional approach during physical intervention. First, it is important that the team leader take charge. This predetermined person can be a behavior specialist, social worker, or classroom teacher. The team leader should orchestrate the physical intervention by making sure that each participant is aware of his or her role before the intervention. Some staff will be better at holding a student's arms; others will prefer to assist with the legs. The team members' roles should be determined before the team enters a room to intervene with a student.

Second, the team leader should give the student the chance to cooperate before the team intervenes. The team leader should tell the student that he or she has a choice: to cooperate within a specified amount of time or to allow staff intervention. The student should be given a verbal warning and should be fully aware of the consequences for noncompliance.

Third, team members should never engage in conversation with a student during a physical episode. The team leader should encourage the student to take his or her time and should tell the student that a staff member will talk with him or her when the student is calm. Should a student try to engage in conversation after his or her time has started, the team leader should give one warning that the time will have to be started over if the student continues to talk. While the student is taking time, the staff should not engage in conversation.

Fourth, whenever possible, physical intervention such as corner, sitting, or floor restraint should not be done in front of other students. It is often preferable to clear a room before restraining a student so that the student will not have an audience to impress. It is also important to teach all class members their responsibility during a crisis. They should understand that they need to refrain from making comments and should continue with their work. It is a good idea to reinforce their appropriate behavior during a crisis.

Fifth, we have found that when a student is exceptionally angry with one staff member, that person should not be a part of the crisis response team. The student's behavior will tend to escalate if that person is involved. After the student is calm, however, that staff member should be involved in bringing the crisis to closure.

Sixth, staff members should know that it is okay, and often wise, to take a break from an intervention if they begin to feel frustrated or angry toward the student. Anger and frustration can lead to poor or hurtful decision-making. Another staff member can step in. Remember that even in physical intervention, staff members are role models for students in appropriate ways of dealing with feelings.

Although physical intervention should be used only as a last resort, there will be times in all schools when students will have to be touched or held to ensure safety. By following the guidelines outlined in this chapter, staff can move toward safe intervention.

▌ DISCUSSION QUESTIONS

1. John is a junior high student who often throws his books in class. No verbal intervention you have tried has worked. You think that he misbehaves in this way to get out of work each day. What physical intervention should you try?
2. You feel that physical intervention is necessary to put an end to the repeated misbehavior of one of your students. How will you go about establishing a crisis response team? Who should be on the team?
3. One staff member "overtalks" whenever a particular stu-

dent becomes disruptive. The overtalking tends to escalate the student's behavior. How can you help this teacher? What can you say to the teacher to explain his or her role in the intervention process? Your explanation should include the time to talk during an intervention and the preferred content of the discussion.

▮ *REFERENCES*

Garrison School Staff. (1994)., *The Garrison Model Handbook*. Garrison School, 936 W. Michigan, Jacksonville, IL 62650.

Johns, B., & Carr, V. (1994). *Safe physical intervention: The Garrison Model for dealing with physical aggression*. Video. Garrison School, 936 W. Michigan, Jacksonville, IL 62650.

BREAKING UP FIGHTS 11

A 1991 Bureau of Justice Statistics report stated that "more than 400,000 students nationwide were estimated to have been victims of violent crimes at school from June 1988 to January 1989" (cited in the National School Safety Center Resource Paper, 1993). The high amount of violence in U.S. schools has led several authors to identify appropriate staff intervention methods for dealing with students who engage in fighting. This chapter provides guidelines for educators based on that information and our own personal experience. The guidelines can assist educators in intervening in a way that will prevent the escalation of aggression and deter verbal aggression from exploding into physical aggression.

As mentioned previously, teachers and school administrators must develop and review with students their expectations for appropriate behavior. The firm, fair, and consistent enforcement of an expectation that clearly states that physical and verbal aggression are unacceptable and the identification of subsequent consequences are vital to deterring aggression.

However, despite the best-laid plans, aggression will occur in the school or on school grounds. According to the *School Safety Check Book* (National School Safety Center, 1990), more teachers and administrators are injured in breaking up fights and assaults than from any other type of activity. We believe that following the guidelines in this chapter will help educators minimize the risk of staff and student injury during intervention.

▎*NEVER OVERLOOK AN AGGRESSIVE ACT*

The first and most important step in reducing recurring violence is to never overlook an aggressive act. Students who use aggression to gain control will act aggressively when they think their actions will be tolerated or overlooked. The teacher or administrator who ignores low-level aggression will increase the likelihood of its recurrence (Gaustad, 1991).

▎*WALK TO THE SCENE OF THE PROBLEM*

Teachers should walk, not run, to a physically or verbally aggressive situation. By running to the scene of a problem the teacher may increase the feeling of tension among those at the scene and may escalate the actions of those involved in the aggressive behavior. On the way to the scene, the teacher may want to stop at another teacher's room to ask for assistance or ask that someone call for assistance.

▎*ASSESS THE SITUATION IMMEDIATELY*

Upon reaching the scene of the aggression, the teacher should quickly assess the problem and begin to develop a plan. A good first step is to identify those students involved with whom the teacher has the best rapport—the students who respond calmly to the teacher. It is important to observe the body stance of the individuals involved in the aggression and be alert to the potential use of weapons. All of these steps should occur in just a few seconds.

Next, the teacher should state assertively that the situation needs to stop. He or she should then call the "watchers, or cheerleaders" who are standing around the scene by name and give them clear directions to leave the area. Statements such as "John, go to Mr. Sanders' room" and "Sally, you need to go to the lunchroom, now" are appropriate. Because the teacher specifies names and areas, there should be no doubts about what is expected.

If time permits, the teacher can mention the penalties for noncompliance with his or her directives. When adult assistance arrives, the teacher can direct one staff member to record the names of those watchers who did not comply. Their parents should later be informed of the incident, and the students should be told that the school will follow up on the situation.

▎ *KEEP AN APPROPRIATE BODY STANCE*

Staff members should not get in between the students involved in the aggression. The student(s) could view that stance as a threat, and the situation could suddenly escalate. Using a technique described in Chapter 6, a staff member should stand in a nonconfrontational manner 1½ to 3 feet away from the aggressive student and at an angle to him or her. Using the students' names, the staff member should repeat the directive, "Stop now." Reminding the students of the consequences of aggression, such as police intervention, is also important. The staff member's tone should be calm, firm, and nonconfrontational.

▎ *IF THE SITUATION HAS NOT COME TO BLOWS, TALK WITH THE STUDENT WITH WHOM YOU HAVE THE BEST RAPPORT*

The staff member should encourage the student with whom he or she has the best rapport to leave the scene and go to a specific place. If the student complies, another staff member should walk with the student. The staff member in charge should then focus on the student who is left and remove him or her to an area separate from the first student. Both staff members should talk with their respective students to bring the situation to closure. Steps for doing so are included at the end of this chapter.

▎ *IF THE INDIVIDUALS ARE ALREADY ENGAGED IN A FIGHT, DIRECT THEM TO STOP AND GET HELP*

The staff member who first arrives at the scene should call the fighters by name and direct them to stop fighting in a firm but low tone. He or she should not intervene physically without assistance. Then the staff member should continue to talk to the students and identify the consequences for their behavior (especially police intervention) until assistance arrives. A statement such as "You need to stop now, our school consequence for hitting is calling the police" is appropriate.

When staff intervene alone, they create a situation for potential injury to themselves or the students and are in a position of being liable. Other adults will serve as witnesses and provide assistance. The best approach for physical intervention is to wait until a trained team is on the scene.

Staff members must be aware of actions that can be misconstrued and may escalate the situation. These include pointing at the aggressor, standing face to face, reaching into the fight, backing a student up to a wall or corner, and yelling. These actions should be avoided at all times.

▮ *DO NOT ALLOW THE AGGRESSOR TO BENEFIT FROM THE AGGRESSION*

It is important to not make the aggressor the center of attention. The staff should draw attention away from the aggressor by attending or talking to the victim first. However, it is also important to not overemphasize one's interaction with the victim. Too much attention to the victim may cause the aggressor to want to "get even" with the victim later. Negative attention, such as yelling and making threats may also encourage further acts of bullying or victimization (Gaustad, 1991).

▮ *ALLOW TRAINED STAFF TO INTERVENE PHYSICALLY*

In our opinion, only members of the crisis response team should touch students acting aggressively. They should act according to the methods outlined in Chapter 9.

▮ *BRING THE SITUATION TO CLOSURE*

After the situation has deescalated, a staff member should talk with the aggressor in private. Public confrontation can enhance the aggressor's status with his or her peers. The staff member should ask who, what, when, and where questions about the situation. Such questions are nonconfrontational and allow students to tell about the situation rather than making them feel the need to blame others.

In the discussion, it is important to emphasize that the school does not tolerate aggression as a means of problem solving. The school expectations and alternative means of problem solving should be discussed; the use of conflict resolution should be encouraged. If the school has set conflict resolution as a mandatory consequence of physical aggression, the aggressor should be told what to expect.

▌ AVOID PHYSICAL PUNISHMENT

We do not favor the use of physical punishment as a consequence for any problem behavior. It sends the conflicting message that students cannot use force for problem solving but adults can. It is better to stress conflict resolution and such consequences as police intervention for battery or assault.

▌ LISTEN TO THE STUDENTS

The staff should listen to the students involved in the aggression both during the incident and during the follow-up discussions. Staff should respond to their appropriate talk in a nonthreatening, matter-of-fact manner.

▌ CONTACT THE PARENTS OF THE "WATCHERS AND CHEERLEADERS"

An important follow-up step is to contact the parents of the "watchers and cheerleaders" who did not comply with the staff's request to leave the scene and inform them of their sons' or daughters' vicarious involvement in the aggressive situation. They should be told the school's stance on violence and observer participation and the penalty for involvement in aggressive behavior. The staff should inform them that the school will enforce the consequences in a firm, fair, and consistent manner and should then do so with the relevant students.

▮ NOTIFY POLICE IN SITUATIONS OF ASSAULT OR BATTERY

Crime in the school should be treated in the same manner as it would be addressed outside of the school—by calling the police. Administrators who do not recognize criminal acts committed in the school as criminal acts are not doing a service to students or the community. They must thoroughly explain to students at the beginning of the school year exactly what constitutes a crime and consistently enforce the expectation that criminal acts will be treated as such. Chapter 12 provides specific details on the use of law enforcement in the school setting.

▮ DOCUMENT THE SITUATION

All incidents must be completely and thoroughly documented. A form like the sample incident report included in the Appendix can be used as a means of recording the situation. If the school presses charges against a student, the form should be copied and sent to the police, the arresting officer, and the state's attorney. In all cases, it should be placed in the student's permanent file. It is important that all staff witnesses participate in the completion of the form to maintain accuracy.

▮ OFFER SUPPORT AND PROTECTION FOR VICTIMS

If bullies continue to act aggressively toward their victims, which they sometimes do, the victims may begin to feel helpless. Students who feel helpless often begin to miss school and avoid interaction. Unfortunately, these behaviors may only encourage the bully to continue his or her aggressive actions. It is important to recognize the victim's feelings and offer some sense of support and perhaps some protection.

▮ DISCUSSION QUESTIONS

1. Think about the last time you were required to break up a fight in your school. How did you handle the situation? Did other adults assist you? Did the aggression of the students who were involved escalate when you came on the scene? Which techniques described in this chapter could you have used to de-escalate the situation.
2. How can you teach your staff to use nonconfrontational methods of intervention when students are verbally or physically aggressive?
3. What expectations and consequences does your school have in place to reduce bullying, verbal aggression, and physical aggression?

▮ REFERENCES

Gaustad, J. (1991). Schools respond to gangs and violence. *Oregon School Study Council Bulletin, 34*. Eugene: University of Oregon.

National School Safety Center. (1990). *School safety check book*. Malibu, CA: Pepperdine University Press.

National School Safety Center Resource Paper. (1993). *Student and staff victimization*. Malibu, CA: Pepperdine University Press.

POLICE INTERVENTION AND COMMUNITY AGENCY INVOLVEMENT 12

■ POLICE INTERVENTION

According to Johns, Carr, and Hoots (in press), students who commit criminal activity in school—including battery, aggravated battery, and criminal damage to property—should face the legal consequence for their crimes. Teachers and administrators are not helping students when they allow them to get away with these activities in school. Further, they are falling short in their responsibility of ensuring that school is a safe environment for all students.

Prior to involving the police in the intervention plan for a school, educators must inform parents and other community members that police intervention will be used. We have been most successful in gaining parental support when we have stressed that the reason for implementing this behavior management procedure is to ensure a safe environment for all students.

Another important preliminary step is to meet and establish a working relationship with members of the police department. Establishing a coordinating council, discussed in more detail later in this chapter, can help facilitate this relationship. As Joan Gaustad (1991) reported, "It is important for schools to have an ongoing relationship with police, rather than just calling on them in the midst of a crisis" (p. 21). One or two individuals in every school building should be designated as the contacts to the police department.

Working with the police, the school must develop a standard operating procedure in writing. The activities that constitute crimes in a school should be specified, and they should be the only activities for which educators call the police. Educators should avoid the dilemma one school district administrator faced. He decided he was going to implement a procedure of police intervention but did not develop a plan with the police. His first official contact with the police was when he called to report that a student was walking up and down the hall being disruptive. He wanted the police to charge the student with disorderly conduct. The police were reluctant to get involved, noting that other interventions for such behavior would be more effective. When the same administrator later called the police to report a major incident that legitimately required police intervention, he had difficulty getting the police to come to the building.

Educators must bear in mind that police will generally not get involved unless an adult has witnessed the crime and is willing to make a statement. It is not enough for one student to say that he or she was hit by another student. If an adult did not see the crime and no adult supervision of the students occurred, there are not grounds for police intervention.

As mentioned previously, any incident that required police intervention should be well documented. An incident report should be completed within twenty-four hours and sent to the police department, the probation department, and the state's attorney; it should also be included in the student's file. We recommend using an incident report similar to that used by the local police. A sample form is included in the Appendix.

Finally, when a student commits a crime and the police are called, the school district should press charges against the student. We cannot overemphasize that allowing the student to get away with the activity will not help, but can only harm, the student.

Police intervention can and will work effectively if educators follow the procedure described here. In this time of increasing violence, educators can no longer work in isolation; they need to establish a working relationship with the police.

In addition to intervening to stop criminal activity, police officers can provide training sessions for students, staff, and parents. They can teach students which activities are considered criminal and will result in charges being pressed and can acquaint them with what will happen if a crime is committed. Of particular relevance today, the police or the school should inform students that possession of any drawings depicting gang activity will be confiscated, marked, dated, and turned over to the police.

The police can train school staff on what constitutes a crime and what constitutes gang activity. They can also provide staff training on drug use and paraphernalia, gang signs, self-defense techniques, illegal contraband, and school security, to name just a few areas.

Police officers can assist in training parents about the signs of possible drug use and gang activity and what to do if children exhibit these signs.

▊ *COMMUNITY AGENCY INVOLVEMENT*

The school district can facilitate community agency involvement in stemming the tide of violence by establishing a coordinating council made up of the agencies and individuals in the area who may work with the students in the school. Included should be members of the police department, the probation department, the city attorney's office, the state attorney's office, the local mental health agency, the family services agency, the truant office, and any other group that provides services to children. Council meetings provide the opportunity for schools to network with the agencies and talk about common problems. They are also helpful for clarifying which agencies are responsible for what activities.

We suggest that schools offer to host the meetings, giving agency representatives an opportunity to be in the schools. Meetings may be held monthly or bimonthly.

In our city, a gang prevention network has also been established. The network consists of members of the police, the probation department, and the school district. The network meets monthly to share information on gang-related issues such as dress and signs.

Gaustad (1991) reported that in a number of communities facing an increase in violence, schools, parents, agencies, and other concerned citizens have banded together to fight crime and organize preventive activities. In Clifton, New Jersey, for example, a master crime prevention plan was developed by a number of agencies, including the school system, the fire department, and the parks and recreation department. According to Gaustad, school systems can effectively work with community groups and parents to develop school-based crime-prevention programs.

■ *DISCUSSION QUESTIONS*

1. Does your school have a working agreement with the local police department?
2. Has police intervention ever been needed at your school? If so, what behaviors warranted a police call?
3. What approach is your school taking to gang problems?
4. Does your school participate on any interagency council? If so, what other groups or individuals participate?

■ *REFERENCES*

Gaustad, J. (1991). *Schools respond to gangs and violence.* (Oregon School Study Council Bulletin No. 34). Eugene: University of Oregon.

Johns, B., Carr, V., & Hoots, C. (in press). *Reduction of school violence: Alternatives to suspension.* Horsham, PA: LRP Publications.

STRATEGIES FOR WORKING EFFECTIVELY WITH PARENTS 13

*T*oo often, teachers blame parents for their children's aggressive behavior and become negative toward them. However, teachers will see greater progress with students if they are able to work cooperatively with the parents. Often, they will need to enlist the parents' help. For these reasons and others, teachers must strive to maintain positive rapport with parents. This chapter describes some effective techniques teachers can use when working with parents.

■ FEEL AND EXPRESS EMPATHY FOR THE PARENT

Teachers need to recognize the stress that a parent faces when raising a child who behaves aggressively. Teachers work with the child for approximately seven hours a day; the parent must deal with the child for the other seventeen. The parent must attend to the child even when he or she is tired and worn-out. Having empathy will assist the teacher in working with the parent.

▮ *POSITIVELY REINFORCE THE STUDENT*

Parents of a child who is aggressive at school become accustomed to receiving negative phone calls from the school. Understandably, they do not look forward to the next phone call. We suggest that teachers break the pattern by calling the parents when their child has had a good day and encouraging them to reinforce the child positively when he or she gets home from school. Alternatively, the teacher can send a note home with the child. It will probably be necessary to tell the child that the note is a positive one; otherwise the child will not want to take it home.

▮ *POSITIVELY REINFORCE THE PARENTS*

It is important for the teacher to thank parents for supporting their behavior management techniques. For instance, if a teacher has a student stay after school to complete an assignment, he or she should be sure to thank the parent for coming to pick up the student. Whenever a parent supports what a teacher is doing in the classroom, the teacher should thank that parent for the support.

▮ *DEFINE SCHOOL EXPECTATIONS*

Teachers should educate parents about their classroom expectations. They should explain the reasons for their rules and the consequences for breaking the rules.

It is often a good idea to invite parents to come into

the classroom to observe the nonconfrontational behavior management techniques being used. Many of the parents have not been using appropriate behavior management at home and will benefit from seeing appropriate techniques in action.

■ PREPARE AND DISTRIBUTE PARENT NEWSLETTERS

Parent newsletters can be very helpful in maintaining good rapport with parents. In them, teachers can openly praise students and their parents by name. For instance, they may recognize those students who have had perfect attendance for the month and thank their parents for getting them to school every day.

■ ESTABLISH A PARENT ADVISORY COUNCIL

We have also found parent advisory councils to be very effective. The council can be convened once a month and should be used as a vehicle for obtaining parental input on school improvement and procedures. The meetings provide parents with an opportunity to be involved in the school in a positive way.

■ ESTABLISH A PARENT SUPPORT GROUP

Parent support groups can provide another opportunity for positive interaction. Discussions in these groups are based on parent needs; the school merely provides the vehicle and setting for the sessions. We have found that parents are most likely to attend meetings when they involve working on projects for the school. For instance, at some meetings at our school, parents have worked on craft projects that they have then sold for the school as fund-raisers. As they worked on the projects, the parents discussed with one another how things were going at home. Serving meals to the parents has also motivated attendance.

▮ *INITIATE PARENTING CLASSES*

Parenting classes are another integral part of an effective school setting. Appropriate topics include, among others, behavior management, building your child's self-esteem, helping your child with homework, and planning summer activities. The key to the success of parenting classes is to have adequate publicity, serve refreshments, and provide a warm, welcoming atmosphere.

School administrators are often discouraged if there are not large turnouts for the classes. But it is important to remember that no matter how many people attend, the classes are meeting the needs of those who do attend.

Often community agencies will offer to teach the classes if the school provides the space. In our area, classes are offered for parents who are having difficulty getting their children to go to school; they are taught by volunteers from the police department, the drug and alcohol treatment center, the truant office, the probation department, and the school.

▮ *DESIGNATE A ROOM IN THE SCHOOL AS A PARENT ROOM*

Parent rooms are becoming more popular. They are places where parents can have a cup of coffee and a cookie and look at literature geared toward meeting their needs. They provide a nonthreatening opportunity for parents to come to school. The parent room should be open to parents at all times during the school day.

■ *ESTABLISH PARENT VISITATION DAY*

Establishing Parent Visitation Day is another good idea for any school. On this day parents can participate in classroom activities and other planned events. In addition to spending time in the classroom, they can meet with ancillary personnel such as the school psychologist and social worker and participate in assemblies on topics such as behavior management. Lunch can be prepared and served by school staff. At our school an awards assembly is held on Parent Visitation Day so parents can see their children being recognized for such accomplishments as perfect attendance, making the honor roll, and excellent bus behavior. Parents also receive awards at the assembly for their involvement in the Parent Advisory Council or other school activities. Our students have been very proud when their parents have received awards.

■ *ESTABLISH A PARENT OPEN HOUSE*

At a Parent Open House, parents come to school to see their child's classroom and meet the teacher. The open house also provides an opportunity for parents to learn more about the policies and procedures of the school. We have found that our open houses are most effective when they have the following components:

1. An opportunity for parents to see their child's classroom or classrooms and meet the teachers.
2. A program about the policies and procedures of the school and the rationale for them. For example, if the

school has adopted a dress code, the dress code and the reason for it should be explained.

3. Refreshments.
4. Family pictures taken and provided to the parents. We do not mean expensive family portraits. At our school's open houses, we have taken family pictures with our own cameras and framed them in cardboard frames on which the school's name has been printed. The portraits have proved to be a motivating attendance factor.

We have also found that attendance increases when we offer incentives such as a pizza party for the class with the greatest percentage of parent attendance.

■ *PROVIDE INFORMATION ABOUT OTHER AGENCIES TO PARENTS*

Many parents with children who are aggressive need support. It is important that educators provide them with information about agencies that are available and the services they provide. For instance, educators can connect parents with counseling services or with child welfare agencies, which can provide homemaker services or respite care for the family. In light of the current thrust to keep children in their own communities, teachers must work with the parents to ensure that they know the community services available to them.

■ *DISCUSSION QUESTIONS*

1. Think about the student in your classroom who exhibits the most aggressive behavior. When was the last time you corresponded with that student's parents about something positive the student did?

2. What opportunities have you given parents to be involved in your classroom or school?
3. What outside support services are available to the parents of the students in your classroom or school?

ADMINISTRATIVE ISSUES *14*

*A*dministrative support is vital for appropriate behavior management intervention in the school setting. It is therefore important that the administration of every school understand and acknowledge the need for such intervention.

Administrators should develop a clearly defined policy for safe physical intervention, and it should be printed in the school handbook for distribution to parents. A sample policy on safe physical restraint and a sample form for documenting its use are included in the Appendix.

If physical intervention is to be considered for students in special education classes, the need for such intervention should be recorded in the student's IEP. A form like the behavior management technique form included in the Appendix can be used to record the techniques suggested for the student. No physical intervention should occur without such a form in place.

We recommend that every school develop a crisis response team to deal with serious verbal and physical aggression. Such teams are called upon when students are out-of-control, and respond in a manner that stresses the safety of all involved. The team should be trained in certified safe physical intervention methods as well as in verbal intervention techniques. We recommend the following steps for establishing and maintaining the crisis response team:

1. Train four to eight staff members in certified safe physical restraint methods.
2. Have all team members attend periodic practices and training sessions to ensure that they remain proficient in the most up-to-date methods.
3. Always have four to five people on the response team (for the safety of all involved). Develop a whole-school code for summoning the team.
4. Teach all faculty about the use of the crisis response team. Be sure to include the following key points: The team should be used only when students are out of control. When the team is called, it should follow through in escorting the student from the area; students should not be allowed to refuse to cooperate until the team is called and then leave the classroom on their own.
5. Develop a whole-school plan that will go into effect when the team is called. The plan should include supervision of team members' classrooms when they are assisting in a crisis.
6. Develop a written, board-approved policy, to be placed in the student handbook, that includes crisis team guidelines, names of team members, types of documentation required, and types of approved intervention. Include a plan for parental notification following the use of physical restraint.
7. Establish written documentation procedures for the use of physical restraint.
8. For students in special education classes, establish pro-

cedures for documenting the possible use of safe physical restraint and time-out as part of the behavior management plan attached to the student's IEP.

We recommend that documentation of physical intervention be placed in the student's temporary and master files. It should also be provided to the student's teacher and legal guardian. If the police or probation office was involved, documentation should be provided to those agencies as well.

Teachers must be accurate and precise when completing this documentation. All forms should be signed and dated. To ensure accuracy, an incident should be recorded no later than at the end of the day during which it occurred.

We advise teachers to take the documentation with them if they are called to testify at a hearing or other legal proceeding. Legal proceedings sometimes are held several months after an incident, and by that time the teacher may have forgotten some of the details. Whether the school prevails at a hearing may depend upon how much written documentation the teacher has and how well the teacher communicates the facts.

Finally, it is important that specific people be designated to inform parents after physical intervention has occurred. A phone call or perhaps a letter may be sufficient for explaining the situation to the parents. It is especially important to inform the parents of students in special education classes of their children's behavior.

▮ *DISCUSSION QUESTIONS*

1. What should the school administration do to assist the school in establishing a crisis response team?
2. How can teachers arrange to cover for colleagues who

are members of the crisis response team when the team is summoned?

3. What type of code call would you recommend for your school? How would you keep teachers from summoning the team unnecessarily?

4. Who do you feel would be ideal members of a crisis response team in your school? Explain why each of these people would be a good addition to the team (personality, style of intervention, attitude toward disruptive students).

APPENDIX

■ SAMPLE PROCEDURAL STATEMENT ON THE USE OF TIME-OUT AS A MANAGEMENT SYSTEM

I. Philosophy:

Time-out from positive reinforcement has proven to be both a widely used and effective technique for suppressing the rate of inappropriate behavior. Time-out procedures have been successfully applied across a variety of behavior problems, situations, and populations. However, effective time-out should be individualized to meet the specific needs of a student as decided by team decision in a Multidisciplinary Conference or a conference called to develop or review the Individualized Education Program. Appropriateness for age, size, and sex of the student is also a team decision.

II. Definition

Operationally defined, time-out refers to the contingent withdrawal of those reinforcing stimuli thought to be maintaining the behavior of interest.

Source: Four Rivers Special Education District, Jacksonville, IL.

III. Purpose

The purpose of time-out is to decrease undesired behavior. Time-out from a positive class environment for preselected, aggressive, destructive, or individually targeted behavior is an effective method for modifying behavior.

IV. Ethical and Legal Considerations

Since time-out procedures may be misused, the following ethical and legal issues shall be addressed before a time-out procedure is employed.

A. A child will be informed regarding the specific behaviors which lead to time-out for him/her prior to using the procedure.
B. After the child completes time-out, the following options will be made available. Scheduling of these procedures would be a team decision on what is most appropriate for the child.
　1. A chance to clarify his/her behavior and the time-out consequence.
　2. A chance to identify and practice alternative behaviors.
C. Parents shall be informed about the use of Level 4 time-out procedures as part of the child's behavior management plan.
D. Records documenting the use of time-out, indicating the name of the student, when the procedure was employed and for how long it was employed, are a mandatory practice of this procedure.

V. Levels

Time-out does not automatically refer to removing the child from the classroom environment. Time-out is used with differing levels of isolation. Four levels will be used.

A. Level 1: Ignoring the child while leaving him/her in the same setting.
Example: The teacher stops reinforcement to the child according to a preselected condition.
B. Level 2: Having the child place his/her head down at his/her desk.
Example: The teacher stops reinforcement to the child by having the child put his/her head on the desk.
C. Level 3: Placing the child apart or separate from the setting in which the target behavior occurs, but within the regular classroom.
Example: Sitting in a corner or isolated in a study carrel.
D. Level 4: Placing the child in a time-out room. The time-out room meets the following minimum qualifications.
   a. Constructed of materials accepted as fire safe by the district or institution. Materials need to be of the same fire-safe materials as used in other parts of the building.
   b. At least four-feet by four-feet floor space with minimum seven-foot ceiling.
   c. Properly lighted.
   d. Properly ventilated.
   e. Free of objects and fixtures with which children could harm themselves.
   f. Having the means by which an adult can continuously monitor, visually and auditorily, the child's behavior.
   g. Unlocked or no door at all.

VI. Parameters

The following conditions will be adhered to when using time-out procedures:

A. Carried out in a matter-of-fact and calm manner.
B. Must occur as an immediate consequence when a pre-defined misbehavior occurs. To maximize opportunities to exercise self-control, the student should be given the opportunity to take his/her own time-out after receiving the instruction from the teacher. However, if the student refuses to take his/her own time-out or if the student fails to respond to the teacher's instruction within a reasonable time interval of 5 to 10 seconds, the teacher should physically remove the student to the time-out area. For high intensity behavior such as kicking, screaming, etc., the student should be immediately escorted to time-out. (It is important that teachers realistically evaluate their ability to physically remove a child to the time-out area. If a pupil is able to break away, the teacher will require assistance.)
C. Accompanied with brief or no discussion, e.g., "Johnny, you cannot stay in the classroom when you _____" or "Because you _____, you must go to time-out for _____ minutes."
D. Be of brief duration. One to five minutes generally is sufficient. It is doubtful that time-out periods exceeding fifteen minutes serve the purpose for which they were intended.
E. Provide for release from time-out contingent upon the student's behavior while in time-out. A change-over delay procedure of one minute (i.e., a contingency for release from time-out of one minute in which no inappropriate responses are omitted) will avoid reinforcing a child's inappropriate behavior while in time-out.
F. Records, as per Section IV.D., should be kept of each occasion when time-out is implemented and should include the following information.

1. The child's name.
2. The episode resulting in the child's placement in time-out.
3. The time of day the child was placed in time-out.
4. The time of day the child was released from time-out.
5. The total time in time-out.
6. The child's behavior in time-out.

VII. Considerations

The multidisciplinary team will evaluate the effectiveness of time-out procedures for each individual child.

■ *SAMPLE TIME-OUT RECORD*

Student's
Name _____   School _____

File Number _____   _____

School Year _____   Teacher _____

Date	Incident	Time In/Out	Behavior in Time-Out

Source: Garrison School Staff (1994).

■ *SAMPLE PROCEDURAL STATEMENT FOR THE USE OF SAFE PHYSICAL RESTRAINT*

Related to Physical Safety of Staff and Students, Severe Behavior Disorders Program

I. Definition

Safe physical restraint is adult physical intervention to hold the student until he or she is calm by exerting physical control that is humane, calm, and, to a large extent, not painful.

II. Purpose

The purpose of safe physical restraint is to prevent a student from self-harm or harm to others and to assist a student who cannot regain self-control after becoming physically aggressive.

III. Ethical and Legal Considerations

The *student will be informed* by the teacher regarding specific behaviors which may lead to physical restraint prior to using the procedure.

After a student has been restrained, the following options will be made available:

1. A chance to clarify his/her behavior and the safe physical restraint consequence.
2. A chance to identify and practice alternative behaviors through the use of life space interviewing.

Parents shall be informed through the Multidisciplinary Conference and/or the Individualized Education Program Conference about the use of safe physical restraint as part of the child's behavior management plan.

Source: Four Rivers Special Education District, Jacksonville, IL.

Records documenting the use of safe physical restraint shall be kept by the teacher. Records shall include:

1. Student's name.
2. The episode resulting in the use of physical restraint.
3. The length of time physical restraint was used.
4. The child's behavior during restraint.
5. The child's behavior following restraint.

IV. Usage

Safe physical restraint may be used with the following situations:

1. When a student exhibits life threatening or physically aggressive behavior to himself or others.
2. When the administration and staff considers the student's behavior extremely disorderly so as to possibly lead to harming the student or others. Some examples include situations in which a student is physically unable to cooperate with staff, such as running through the hallway, hitting classroom windows or doors without stopping, throwing objects or furniture without stopping, or continuing to damage school equipment or furniture.

V. Procedures for Use of Physical Restraint

All staff will be trained in the techniques of safe physical restraint.

The situation will be handled in a matter-of-fact and calm manner.

The teacher or adult in charge should first involve the student in conversation designed to calm the student and extinguish physically aggressive behavior.

The teacher or adult in charge should initiate physical contact, when appropriate, such as "hand on shoulder" while instructing the student in a calm manner to report to the quiet room or designated area or to stop the inappropriate behavior.

When additional adult assistance is needed, at least four adults should be involved in the encounter to insure the safety of the staff and the student. One adult will direct the encounter. Usually that adult will be the behavior specialist or teacher.

The following steps will be taken when using safe physical restraint:

1. To maximize opportunities to exhibit self-control, students will be given the opportunity to stop their own behavior with a verbal comment/warning from the teacher, which will also give the student options of appropriate alternative behavior.
2. If the student fails to respond within a reasonable time interval of 5 to 10 seconds, the directions will be repeated and the student will be notified that if he does not cooperate he will be physically restrained or removed from the situation.
3. One adult will direct the encounter. Safe restraint methods will be employed to restrain with one adult holding each leg and each arm. The student will be held until he is calm and under control.
4. Once the student is calm the adult in charge will talk calmly with the student to help him/her:
   a. Identify the student's feelings that led to the inappropriate behavior.
   b. Identify the inappropriate behavior and its consequences.
   c. Identify appropriate behaviors and consequences for use in similar situations.
5. Duration of restraint will be only as long as necessary for the student to become calm.

VI. Considerations

The multidisciplinary team will evaluate the effectiveness of safe physical restraint procedures for each individual child.

■ *SAMPLE POLICE INCIDENT REPORT*

INCIDENT REPORT/STUDENT: _____

FILE # _____ DATE _____

J. arrived at 8:30 a.m. from his bus. Mr. D. saw J. hit Nancy in the back of the head as J. walked toward school from the bus. As J. entered the school he began yelling. His teacher, Mrs. R., came to the door. She spoke with J. and offered time-out as a means to get calm. J. stated that he could follow the class rules and showed Mrs. R. his white slip from the bus. (The driver did not see the hit as J. left the bus; Mrs. R. did not know about the hit at this time.) J. went to class.

Mr. D. told Mrs. R. that he witnessed the hit as J. got off the bus and it was determined that J. should go to time-out. Mrs. R. asked J. to go to time-out. Although he complained, he walked on his own and remained calm while facts were being gathered.

Mrs. C. spoke with J. He denied any problems on or off the bus. She explained that Mr. D. had witnessed the incident and saw J. hit Nancy in the back of the head. At this time J. was sitting in the back of the time-out room, and Mrs. R. and Mrs. C. were standing at the doorway of the room facing J. Mr. D. stepped behind Mrs. R. and Mrs. C. J., who had been calmly sitting, saw Mr. D., lurched forward, and began screaming and yelling. He stated that he did not touch Nancy, that everybody picks on him, and that he did not do anything. He suddenly ran toward the doorway, lunged out, and punched Mr. D. in the chest. He intentionally raised his middle knuckle to intensify the punch. Mrs. R. and Mrs. C. held his arms and began to pull him backward off Mr. D. and into the time-out room.

Mrs. W. heard the yelling and came into the room to assist. J. kicked her in the chest with all his strength and knocked her into the wall and onto the floor. J. was then restrained on the floor. However, he tried to head-butt Mrs. R. repeatedly. Mrs. C. held his head. At that time he tried to bite Mrs. C. The entire incident took place in one minute or less. However, even after the incident, J. continued to make threats to kill or hurt Mr. D.

J. became somewhat calm after about three to five minutes of restraint. He was released, and the Jacksonville Police were called. Probation was notified. Officer B. came to the school, and J. was taken to the Jacksonville Police Station. I spoke with Mrs. P., the juvenile probation officer, and J.'s parents were notified.

Mrs. W. went to Passavant Hospital. Upon examination she was found to be badly bruised in the chest and back. The doctor prescribed Tylenol with codeine. She was also advised to rest at home for at least two days.

Signed: (Teacher; Adults involved)

cc: Officer Brown, Jacksonville Police Dept.
    C. Petefish, Morgan County Juvenile Probation
    Morgan County State's Attorney
    Master file/Teacher file

■ *SAMPLE PHYSICAL RESTRAINT RECORD*

Student's
Name _____   School _____

File Number _____   _____

School Year _____   Teacher _____

Behavior During/After

Date	Incident	Time	Physical Restraint

_____

Source: Garrison School Staff (1994).

▮ *SAMPLE BEHAVIOR MANAGEMENT TECHNIQUE FORM FOR STUDENTS IN SPECIAL EDUCATION CLASSES*

Student_____ IEP Date_____ File #_____

Behavior Management Techniques
(least to most restrictive)

_____ Positive reinforcement
_____ Classroom management system
_____ Level of system (indicate entry level____, star system____, point system____)
Indicate individual behavior concerns for level of system:

_____

_____

Contracting (focus on incentives for appropriate behaviors)

integration contract____, work completion contract____, drivers education contract____, attendance contract____, general contracting as needed____

_____ White slips for appropriate behavior on the bus
_____ Earned free time or snack
_____ Conflict resolution/peer mediation
_____ Climate committee referral
_____ Delayed lunch/dine on time
_____ Shortened day
_____ Extended day—after school due to excessive noncompliance
_____ Finishing work after school when work refusal occurs
_____ Audio- and videotaping in the classroom
_____ Audio- and videotaping on the bus

_____ Positive alternative learning environment (PALE) at Garrison School___ at home school___
_____ Time-out
_____ Safe physical restraint/protection when head-banging
_____ In-school restitution for damage to property
_____ Cleaning restroom when spitting occurs
_____ Plans, as needed, to be coordinated by the behavior management specialist and teacher

Others: _____

_____

Signed _____ Position _____

■ *SAMPLE INCIDENT REPORT*

Student_____ File #_____ Date _____

Age_____ DOB_____ Address _____

Parent/Guardian _____

Address_____

Victim_____ Age_____ DOB _____

Adult Witness(es)—Name/Position _____

_____

_____

Date/Time of Incident _____

Location of Incident _____

Type of Incident_____

Injuries/Damage _____

Object of Incident (Assault, Theft, Etc.) _____

_____

Method (Hit with Fist, Threw Object, Etc.)_____

_____

Officer Involved _____

Narrative (Write Exactly What Student and Victim Said or Did During the Incident; Give Specific Details of Incident):

_____

_____

_____

_____

_____

_____

_____

_____

_____

_____

_____

Report Made By _____

Position_____

Date _____

School_____

School Address _____

▮ *SAMPLE CLASSROOM MANAGEMENT PLAN*

Classroom Expectations

1. Follow directions the first time given.
2. Be inside the classroom with all necessary materials by the time the bell rings.
3. Refrain from interrupting when someone else is addressing the class.
4. Refrain from bringing any food or drink into class.
5. Follow all lab safety rules included in the lab safety contract.

Positive Consequences

1. Praise.
2. "No Homework" pass the next day if all work is completed the previous day.
3. Positive comments on grade cards.
4. Positive phone call or note written home for weekly appropriate behavior.

Negative Consequences

1. Warning.
2. Stay after class 5 minutes.
3. Stay after class 8 minutes.
4. Referral for Saturday school.
5. Request parent conference.

▍ *GARRISON SCHOOL EXPECTATIONS*

1. School doors open at 8:30 a.m.
2. Students will follow the transportation as required by their IEP.
3. Students will maintain 90% attendance, unless IEP states otherwise, in order to successfully pass a quarter.
4. Students will leave tape players and tapes at home.
5. Students will bring completed forms for medication to be given at school.
6. Students will refrain from bringing cigarettes, lighters, matches, chewing tobacco, and related items on the bus or to school.
7. Students will refrain from bringing any inappropriate or dangerous items on the bus or to school.
8. Students will refrain from aggressive behavior on the bus and in the school.
9. Students will remain at school for the entire school day.
10. Students will be in the halls only with permission.
11. Students will be escorted to the restrooms by staff members.
12. Students will be responsible for restitution if property is damaged or destroyed.

Students will be fully informed of the school rules and consequences by their teachers.

Source: Garrison School Staff (1994).

▮ *GARRISON MAJOR INFRACTIONS 1993–94*

1. Verbal aggression that requires outside intervention.
2. Physical aggression to staff or peers.
3. Stealing.
4. Destruction or infringement of property.
5. Possession of contraband at school.
6. Any behavior resulting in a police call.
7. Smoking at school.
8. Spitting.
9. Walking out of the classroom without permission.
10. Requiring the team escort to leave classroom.
11. Repeated and deliberate dress code violation.

Violation of these whole school major infractions will result in a drop of all levels.

Source: Garrison School Staff (1994).

▍ *LUNCHROOM EXPECTATIONS*

1. Students will walk.
2. Students will remain seated unless they are cleaning their area.
3. Students will use low voice level.
4. Students will clean up their area when finished eating.
5. Students will follow the directions of the adults on lunch duty.
6. Students will be given only one warning regarding rules—a second request will result in a zero.
7. Students who have work to finish will complete work at a designated table.

Source: Garrison School Staff (1994).

■ RESOURCES FOR EDUCATORS

Publications

Beck, M., Coleman, T., & Wineman, D. (1985). *Managing the unmanageable student*. Lexington, MA: Ginn Press.

Cummins, K. (1988). *The teacher's guide to behavioral interventions*. Columbia, MO: Hawthorne Educational Services.

Davis, R. W. (1988). *Therapeutic management of anger and aggressive behavior*. Valdosta, GA: Accelerated Human Development.

DeBruyn, R., & Larson, J. (1984). *You can handle them all*. Manhattan, KS: The Master Teacher.

Gallagher, P. (1988). *Teaching students with behavior disorders*. Denver: Love.

Gaustad, J. (1990). *Gangs* (ERIC Digest Series No. EA 52). Eugene, OR: ERIC Clearinghouse on Educational Management (ERIC Document Reproduction Service No. ED 321 419).

Gaustad, J. (1991). *Schools attack the roots of violence* (ERIC Digest No. 63, EDO-EA-91-5). Eugene, OR: ERIC Clearinghouse on Educational Management (ERIC Document Reproduction Service No. ED 335 806).

Gaustad, J. (1991). Schools respond to gangs and violence. *Oregon School Study Council Bulletin, 34*. Eugene: University of Oregon.

Goldstein, A., Harootunian, B., & Conoley, J. (1994) *Student aggression*. New York: Guilford Press.

Goldstein, A., & Huff, C. (1993). *The gang prevention handbook*. Champaign, IL: Research Press.

Guetzloe, E. (1989). School prevention of suicide, violence, and abuse. *Education Digest, 55,* 46–49.

National School Safety Center. (1991). *Gangs in schools— breaking up is hard to do.* Malibu, CA: Pepperdine University Press.

National School Safety Center. (1990). *School safety check book.* Malibu, CA: Pepperdine University Press.

National School Safety Center News Service. (1991, November). *School Safety Update,* pp. 1–8.

National School Safety Center News Service. (1992, March). *School Safety Update,* pp. 1–6.

Schrumpf, F. (1991). *Peer mediation.* Champaign, IL: Research Press.

Sprick, R. (1985) *Discipline in the secondary classroom.* West Nyack, NY: The Center for Applied Research in Education.

Walker, J., & Shea, T. (1988) *Behavior management: A practical approach for educators.* Columbus, OH: Merrill.

Wood, M., & Long, N. (1991). *Life space intervention.* Austin, TX: PRO-ED.

Associations

Council for Children with Behavioral Disorders. Council for Exceptional Children, 1920 Association Drive, Reston, VA 22091, 703-620-3660.

National Crisis Prevention Institute. 3315-K N. 124th St., Brookfield, WI 53005, 800-558-8976.

INDEX